DILEMMAS of URBAN AMERICA

The Godkin Lectures at Harvard University · 1965

*The Godkin Lectures on the Essentials of
Free Government and the Duties of the Citizen
were established at Harvard University in 1903
in memory of Edwin Lawrence Godkin (1831-1902).
They are given annually under the auspices of the
Harvard Graduate School of Public Administration.*

DILEMMAS of URBAN AMERICA

ROBERT C. WEAVER

HARVARD UNIVERSITY PRESS

Cambridge · Massachusetts · 1966

Distributed in Great Britain by Oxford University Press, London

Library of Congress Catalog Card Number: 65–22056

Printed in the United States of America

To the memory of Catherine Bauer Wurster

PREFACE

THIS BOOK IS based on the Godkin Lectures which I delivered at Harvard University the last three evenings of March 1965.

During the four years I have been in Washington, I have spoken at universities and colleges at least a score of times annually. Like most who have been in the classroom, I have a nostalgia to return, if only occasionally. But my primary motive has been to revel in a setting where I can put away—for a time—the operations of an agency and substitute the process of problem formulation and analysis.

The Godkin Lectures, with their sixty-year tradition and the ample amount of time they allow the speaker on the stage, provide a unique opportunity to formulate basic issues. The give and take during the question period affords additional exposure and discussion. Despite the fact that there were some unexpected developments during the question period, most of the colloquy last March centered upon the concepts and general philosophy of my lectures.

Thus if Godkin Lectures contribute something to the university community—and I must assume that they do— in my case the preparation and delivery of the lectures contributed a great deal more to me. And to me it is altogether fitting that I undertook this analysis at the university where, some thirty years ago, I completed my undergraduate and graduate training.

Public administration is popularly conceived of as action-oriented. And, too often, it is just that and no more. Action without program, problem solving without problem analysis, day-by-day decisions without a philosophy are a travesty of public administration. They are inexcusable and dangerous in the modern world where public policy is so vital to the well-being of all citizens.

These observations cause no controversy in a university setting and find general acceptance once articulated, but doing something about the situation does cause difficulties to administrators. The pressures to get things done are overwhelming. One has to secure necessary legislation, obtain adequate appropriations, assemble, keep, and utilize effectively a competent staff, interpret programs, and perform a multiplicity of anticipated functions, as well as resolve a large volume of emergency situations. These responsibilities leave little time and reduced energy for analyzing the philosophy that underlies action.

Those who, like myself, have addressed themselves to such analysis in the past, sometimes tend to assume that they have accumulated a thought bank which will sustain them for all time. One of the surest ways to extricate oneself from this form of delusion is to contemplate lecturing before a university community. There the audience is composed primarily of persons who are continually formulating and challenging the philosophy which, consciously or unconsciously, provides the rationale for administrative action.

As it turned out, my audiences at Harvard were composed partly of citizens from nearby communities who had little concern for philosophy but held definite views about local developments. Thus, when urban renewal was discussed, their presence and participation made the question period quite lively. (I was told that seldom had it been as heated.) Unfortunately the tone of that colloquy cannot be reproduced here; I mention it only to suggest that the subject matter of this book is of great concern to many and diverse elements in the population.

This volume is far from being a mere transcript of the lectures as delivered. I have expanded the manuscript, rewritten much of it, added illustrative materials and supporting data, reorganized the chapters on urban renewal and dilemmas of race, and in some instances taken account of later developments. In the process I have benefited from the perceptive editorial suggestions of Mr. Max Hall of Harvard University Press.

R.C.W.

Housing and Home Finance Agency
Washington, D.C.
June 1965

CONTENTS

Dilemmas of Urban America

1

URBANIZATION

Seven out of ten people in the United States live in
urban areas, and by 1970 the proportion will be even
greater. Our technology has enabled us to produce more
and more farm products with less and less farm manpower, so that those living on farms are decreasing
absolutely and relatively. We are in fact, though perhaps
not in our thinking or in our governmental institutions, an
urban people. Our most pressing problems result from
our urbanism.

But, as a comparatively young nation which finds much
of its most glorious tradition and unique philosophy in
terms of an agricultural past, we often manifest a cultural
hangover. Even Thomas Jefferson, the champion of the
common man, feared the city mob so much that he
wanted no large urban concentrations of the population.
This anti-city philosophy manifests itself today in our
propensity to view the city as a symbol of evil and cor-
ruption. Thus, there is a tendency to revel in a glorifica-
tion of the "good old days."

We are, of course, slowly lifting this veil of doctrine
as we are forced to face reality. For me, it is somewhat

ironic that the Supreme Court, so often the preserver of the past, has recently, in its reapportionment decisions, become the prime agency for accelerating a realization of our urban present.

The word "urban" as used here means the city and its surrounding concentrations of population. Urbanization implies a diminution of the importance of agriculture and a growth of industrialization. Today it occurs at a time when there is a shift from heavy, dirty production to light, clean production. It finds expression, also, in a significant rise in the number and proportion of the labor supply concentrated in highly skilled, professional, research, clerical, and service pursuits. It refers to a society in which future growth in manpower requirements will continue to reflect a lesser need for farm labor, a significant relative decline in the demand for untrained workers, a consistent concentration of our people in and around cities, and the inevitable expansion of metropolitan areas.

In such a society, we face problems of land utilization and development, problems of conserving and revitalizing our existing areas of population concentration, and adjustments incident to the relationships between human beings who are in varying degrees of proximity one to the other. All of these problems arise in a new milieu. As contrasted to the relatively simple life of several generations ago, urban living today involves a complex of activities in which the individual and the family become increasingly dependent upon community action as contrasted to individual action. This dependence may manifest itself in the need for such mundane things as garbage collection, or it may find expression in complicated laws and administration having to do with zoning and building codes. It may become operative in the provision and regulation of parking facilities, or it may involve the planning and construction of highways and rapid transit facilities. Inevitably urban living presents problems of education, employment, and welfare, which usually occasion public policy and public action.

James Reston recently observed that "in a fit of exuberance or absent-mindedness we have increased the population of the United States by over 50 million since 1945." [1] As we all know, the exuberance and absent-mindedness of which Reston spoke are continuing, and at such a pace that by the time the children of the last fifteen years are grandparents, there may be another 125 million or so people in this nation. A population of some 300 million is projected for the turn of the century, and at least 85 percent of it will reside in urban areas.

This growth is the most portentous single fact of our time—always excepting the thermonuclear threat. It means, among other things, that in the next thirty-five or forty years we may have to build as much housing, industrial plants, and highways as we have built in our previous history. In the process, the amount of land consumed by urbanization will be doubled.

2
NEW COMMUNITIES

T HE TREMENDOUS population surge of the next thirty-
five years will be accommodated largely in what we now
consider the metropolitan fringe, and, in many cases, in
undeveloped or agricultural lands even farther removed
from existing concentrations of population. Already
metropolitan growth has produced phenomena variously
known as "Spread City," "urban sprawl," and "slurbs."
Though we have done a remarkable job of housing a
growing population in structures which quantitatively,
and often qualitatively, are impressive, the resulting urban
environment leaves much to be desired. Not only has
ugliness botched land uses, but the process has been
extremely wasteful. Basic community facilities, such as
water and sewer systems, have been often inadequate, and
all too frequently built on a piecemeal, too-little-too-late
basis. Roads and highways have been developed with little
thought to their repercussions on future land-use patterns,
and commercial and industrial buildings have gone up
willy-nilly, wherever a local zoning ordinance could
be obligingly bent. In other instances residential enclaves
have fought against industrial development at the outset

only to mature and find that their earlier action deprived the community of a vital supplementary tax base. We have suburbs which are lacking in cultural facilities and harassed by schools that have not expanded to match population increases—suburbs which remain inaccessible to the service workers who are so sorely needed.

These criticisms are familiar. There is, however, another feature of our land use which has been less frequently articulated. The tendency in the past has been to bulldoze down trees and pleasant rolling land contours in a hurried effort to build as quickly, and often as cheaply, as possible. Not only does this violate nature but it seems to me to violate logic as well. For it destroys some of the very attributes which are supposed to recommend suburban living—a return to open spaces and enjoyment of the beauties of the countryside. This haphazard development has left us with a considerable deficit, in terms of the physical condition of many of our suburban communities and particularly in terms of their capacity to accommodate future growth.

In the midst of a certain amount of physical chaos, there has developed such a social uniformity as to provide ammunition for pundits and philosophers. Oscar Handlin writes, "What is new [in the long-term movement to the suburbs] is the effective motivation—the insistence upon constructing small, uniform, coherent communities, and the surrender of the adventure of life in the larger units with all the hazards and opportunities of unpredictable contacts." [1]

Actually, of course, many residents in suburbia have

found much of what they sought when they moved away from the city. For them there is comfort and identification in Herbert Gans' words: "Most of the people who have written about suburbia come—like other writers—from the cosmopolite upper middle class. Their criticism of suburban life is actually directed at working- and lower middle-class, non-cosmopolite ways, which can be found in most city neighborhoods as well, but are not as visible there as they are in suburbia." "The myth of suburbia," according to Gans, "is only a contemporary variation on a theme that has been prominent in American critical writing for many decades." [2]

To me, Handlin, to a lesser degree, and Gans, to a significant degree, appear to have over-intellectualized the situation. Many Americans have never enjoyed the "adventure of life in the larger units" to which Handlin refers.[3] And this is brought home when I visit small college towns and listen to those who grew up in New York City. They are the true proponents of "small, uniform, coherent communities," and I get the impression that they would withdraw into such a community regardless of where they lived. Pressures for social uniformity are not restricted to suburbia; nor are they unknown in central cities.

Perhaps, in their unconscious, some of the critics of suburbia reflect the values of the "cosmopolite upper middle class," but many of the characteristics they attribute to suburbia are the trademarks of suburbs. The cultural attributes of suburbia and central cities are a reflection of personal preferences as well as physical and social environments. No doubt each environment exerts an influence towards particular values and conduct, but in a society where there is a high degree of mobility for most urban dwellers, individual preferences go far in determining the types of communities we elect to live in.

I suggest that the lure of the suburbs is basically no different from the motivation that underlies all migration: the push of the defects of the environment from which the migrant moves and the pull of the attractiveness of the place to which he goes. In many instances the "pull" may be no more subtle than a desire for a yard in which children can play, a place where there can be a garden, and an opportunity for home ownership. As in all migration, the movement to suburbia in this nation has resulted in realization of hopes and in disappointment.

In the controversy over the relative merits of the suburb, each individual has to make his own choices. Apparently, this is exactly what the American people have been, and are, doing. From what one can observe, there is far from a universal, monolithic judgment. And for many persons, choices vary at different periods in an individual's age span, reflecting the relative advantages that suburbs and central cities afford.

There is, however, a by-product of suburbia which complicates our urban living. It is the dichotomy in identification between the suburbs and the central cities. This dichotomy is a linear descendant of the traditional urban-rural conflict. For as William H. Whyte observed, "long before there were suburbs there was a rural-urban conflict. A persistent theme in utopian literature has been the basic immorality of cities and the coupling of the good life with the rural virtues." [4] As a consequence, there is too little willingness to identify the problems of city and suburb as parts of a single metropolitan problem. Neither growth in the metropolitan fringes nor decay in the older areas of the central city can be conveniently sorted out and considered alone. The two components of the metropolitan complex are interdependent; and if one questions this, let him consider for a moment the matter of transportation. It, like so many other urban problems, does not stop at the geographic limits of local governments nor can its solutions fail to cross these proliferated lines of political control.

Regardless of the merits or defects of our present suburbs, we shall have more of them in the future. The issue we face, therefore, is not a choice of whether or not we construct more housing in the fringe areas and beyond, but whether or not we can do so in a more creative, economic, and aesthetically attractive manner.

PEOPLE'S ASPIRATIONS

Before there can be meaningful discussion of the instrument, or the instruments, which could best improve suburban living, it will be necessary to consider briefly the structure of suburbia. Given our technical knowhow, our natural resources, and our general affluence, to what sort of suburbs could we aspire? What human values are important and what physical arrangements could facilitate them? This calls for more than a catalogue of what is right and what is wrong with suburbia today;

and it is less than the development of Utopia. It is complicated by the fact that we are a heterogeneous population, living in a society which prides itself on freedom of choice and wide opportunities for consumer preferences.

What we want is, in no small measure, determined by what we can envision. And what we can envision is conditioned by what we dream as well as what we see. As a people, who are, for the most part, socially and economically mobile, we have a tendency to accept the established, to question the novel, and to resist the unknown. For mobility creates insecurity, and insecurity breeds conservatism. Nowhere is this more apparent than in shelter. A home is the most costly possession of most Americans and one of their basic symbols of status. The building industry and financial institutions, partly because of these tendencies and partly because of their own conservatism, develop an inertia against innovation. Thus, although it is relatively easy to list the defects of our present housing and community facilities, it is quite difficult to prescribe the ideal.

But there are certain things that cannot be left out of consideration. There are amenities which are consistent with comfort and efficiency. There are principles of site design which make for safe and satisfying patterns of living. The location of our housing concentrations and their relationships one to the other and to the central city influence the ease with which we can travel within and throughout the urban complex and the extent to which we make nature available to our people. Design, both of communities and the elements in them, determines the aesthetics of our environment.

All are interrelated and, in turn, are influenced by the arrangements we make for transportation, open spaces, and communications. The life that exists in any neighborhood or community is of course, determined, in large part, by the composition of the population which lives in it. Also, it is affected by the economic character of the area. A bedroom suburb nurtures certain cultural patterns, values, and conduct which tend to differ from those that blossom forth in a community where most residents find employment as well as shelter within its borders.

Suburbs are deeply affected by transportation facilities. Indeed, the rise of suburbia of this nation owes something to the railroad industry, despite the more recent abandonment of the industry's concern for commuters. Half a century ago the railroads found themselves with underutilized lines and abundant land grants. Some of them nurtured the concept of suburban living and contributed greatly to the national image of the joys and virtues of living closer to nature. Subsequently the streetcar and the bus facilitated more extensive suburban living.

Today the automobile influences significantly the structure of the suburbs—and to a remarkable degree the central city. It has greatly expanded the possibilities of suburban living, contributing to the scatteration which now plagues our land. Also, the automobile has led to the growing need for highways, freeways, and turnpikes, all of which eat up urban land, at the same time that they influence, if not dictate, the location of housing. No practical solution to urban land use can be envisioned that fails to take into account the automobile and other forms of transportation.

There is no one pattern of suburbia that will satisfy the needs and aspirations of all our people. In addition, these aspirations are not static; they are, however, in large measure limited by the existing patterns and arrangements which the people can see and experience. This means that we must not only think and talk about better environments but also create them. We will have to experiment. We will have to build models.

By "we," I mean both government and private industry. In our economy, there are basic roles for both, as well as for joint efforts involving both.

In order to embark upon this activity intelligently, we need to establish a theoretical basis for our actions. This requires utilization of our best thinking, and it requires careful discussion and debate. But we cannot wait until the discourse is completed before we begin to experiment. Indeed, the need for more housing will assure expansion in home building and urban development; the opportunity is to guide them into new expressions that may better serve the needs and meet the aspirations of the American public.

In all of this no element is fixed. Man's needs change and his concepts of them change, often at a less rapid pace. Taste and preferences are variable, too. And each new form or arrangement in the physical settings in which we live, in turn, changes our perspectives and influences our tastes and preferences.

It is in such a dynamic frame of reference that we must consider proposals for better forms of urban living. Although there is some degree of consensus as to what we want—more comfort, more beauty, greater efficiency, and environments that maximize happiness and satisfaction—we have not yet discovered, and probably never will discover, the optimum arrangement. Indeed, there are probably a series of such patterns. Meanwhile, as we broaden our choices, our objectives will shift. Although there are no definitive solutions, we know that we can have a better environment. Like mankind everywhere, we are seeking to achieve it.

Our generation is blessed in that for most of us, the problems of acute scarcity and poverty no longer exist. For those who still experience poverty, we are embarking upon efforts to eliminate it. We are capable of producing enough not only to sustain and improve our standard of living but to provide also sufficient food, clothing, and shelter for all in this nation and many elsewhere.

As a people so endowed, we are tempted to concentrate upon a solution that will supply the answer to all our problems. We seek a formula that will, at once, be logical, simple, and satisfying. If it is one that exists elsewhere, so much the better. For, as a practical people, we can point to it and thereby identify a prototype that all can see and emulate. But sometimes we get a little overenthusiastic about the prototype.

NEW TOWNS

In an effort to achieve more rational land use, ethnically and economically diversified new developments, and more attractive environments, there has been a tendency to look for *the* solution. For suburbia, the most popular answer among some planners and liberals seems to be "new towns."

These are primarily a European institution, concentrated in Great Britain and Scandinavia. They are well-planned large communities, usually removed from existing cities, providing housing accommodations, employment opportunities, and public, educational, and cultural facilities, as well as commercial amenities. They are usually planned, executed, and owned by a governmental entity. In most of the European new towns the residents find employment, social life, and housing within the borders of the development.

Regretfully, one notes that much that has been written on the subject in this country describes European experience and then proposes a reproduction of it in the United States. Without going into details at this point, let it be noted that we cannot successfully recreate in this nation approaches and programs which have evolved out of a somewhat different European environment. Recognition of this fact led me a year ago to speak of "new communities" rather than "new towns" in America.

In 1953 the Bowery Savings Bank published a pamphlet on *The English New Town.* Its purpose was "to invite attention to the British experiment by those officially concerned with housing matters and especially by the government mortgage insurance agencies and the institutions financing such insured mortgages." With rare perception the article stated: "The methods followed in the British experiment are not put forward as a pattern for adoption in the United States. The British historical background and political philosophy differ too greatly from the American tradition and viewpoint . . . But while we may disagree with British methods, it is possible at the same time to sympathize with their objectives and respect their achievements." [5] Unfortunately, much of the current American discussion about new towns has ignored these warnings sounded over a decade ago.

Not only is there uncritical espousal of the European new-town concept, but there is also a reliance upon that instrument as the suburban cure-all for our urban explosion. In a nation where fads are popular, this was perhaps inevitable; yet such a fad has more serious implications than most others. Overemphasis upon new towns, as a solution to urban sprawl and as *the* form of future suburban development, could well divert our attention from more fundamental and comprehensive approaches.

This is no figment of my imagination. Albert Mayer, for example, said recently that new towns in America would require a public, government-backed body to acquire and retain the land. The resulting communities would be to a maximum extent self-contained, as far as daily operations are concerned. Thus, Mr. Mayer, who clearly states that he has drawn heavily from British and Swedish experiences, proposes new towns as the ideal form of suburban development. He would look to new towns—both newly created and formed by the enlargement of existing suburban communities—as the principal instrument for meeting the housing needs of the impending population explosion in the United States.[6]

Dennis O'Harrow, executive director of the American Society of Planning Officials, is unequivocal. As the title of his recent article on the subject suggests, the issue for him is "New Towns or New Sprawl?" [7] He affirms that large-scale developments are inevitable and "if they are not to be sprawl, they must be reasonably self-sufficient and self-contained. They will then be 'new towns' in the English sense." This doctrinaire approach is reinforced by the statement "there is still another essential for a proper new town. This is that *from its very beginning* the new town must have a clearly stated maximum size and some assurance that the maximum will be respected." Finally, Mr. O'Harrow concludes that "government and only government is the proper agency to assume the initiative and responsibility for producing our future urban nation," a position, of course, with which Albert Mayer would concur and one which follows English precedents. I encountered this article just as I had finished reading an impressive study of the new-town movement in Great Britain. It, too, had a significant title, *The New Towns, The Answer to Megalopolis*.[8]

English new towns were designed to deal with problems which had long harassed English cities. Among these were the enormous size of London and its tendency to continue to grow. Also, the increasing concentration of industry in the southern part of the island had occasioned concern and dissatisfaction. The British, long before Americans and with a more unswerving passion, pined for individual, free-standing cottages with gardens. Thus, it was natural that the garden-city concept of Ebenezer Howard would provide a workable vehicle to meet the needs. Lewis Mumford has summarized well the essence of Howard's theory, saying: "Howard's first great contribution to the new towns movement was his conception that the parts of a city were in organic relation to each other, and that there was accordingly a functional limit to the growth of any one element, as to the growth of the whole. Using London as the classic example of disorganized overgrowth, he sought to relieve the pressure of congestion by colonizing its excess of population in new centres, limited in area and population." [9] But Howard, unlike some of his disciples, did not stop with the concept that a single garden city or a scattering of them would be adequate. Rather he envisioned, according to Mumford, "the creation of a regional unit that would bring into a single organized system at least ten cities with a total population of three hundred thousand, bound together by a rapid public transportation system that would unify the cities and make them operate, for any purpose that involved all of them, as a single unit." [10]

In modern Britain new towns have been created, in part, to put an end to cities' (especially London's) positive increase in over-all employment capacity and total population. [11] Thus, the new-towns program was designed to effect a significant displacement of population. [12] Basic to this program are assertions that cities are now by common consent too large and national government action is required to limit their size.[13] At the same time, it was recognized that control of the location of employment is the key to population redistribution. To deal with the problems which faced Great Britain it was necessary to accept the idea of a national planning authority of some kind and the creation of a system of land-use control and a machinery for town construction.[14] Thus the New Towns Act of 1946 provided for the creation of *ad hoc* development corporations, appointed and financed by the National Ministry of Town and County Planning. It was these bodies which developed the recent new towns —developments which are aptly described as Government New Towns.[15]

Through government loans to the government-created corporations, it has been possible to place land ownership in the public sponsor and have the latter lease it to tenants. This was facilitated to a marked degree by the English precedents in the practices of aristocratic landowners who also retained land ownership and permitted tenants to occupy it under various arrangements.

Little analysis is required to indicate that our problems differ from those which harassed England, that our traditions and instruments of government are not comparable to those of the English, and that we have no such precedents in land tenure.

Whereas feudalism gradually gave way to the manorial system, which is the backbone of the precedent for leaseholdings in England, the tradition of land tenure differed in the New World. One of the inducements to migration to America, even in colonial times, was the possibility of economic opportunity. And in that agricultural era, land ownership was a key element in economic status. Yet at first there were so few settlers and so much land that the settlers refused to pay either purchase price or rent for it. As Marion Clawson has written, "The idea of unrestricted land ownership, in sharp contrast to feudal land tenures, was widely held by the time of the Revolution, and it was to dominate American land history for a century or more afterward." [16]

This concept of unrestricted land ownership was reinforced during the long era of public land disposal. For it must be remembered that over two thirds of the total area of the forty-eight contiguous states has been public domain at one time or another, and in the nineteenth century we disposed of more than two thirds of the public land, or more than half of the total land area of the United States. No wonder this disposal activity dominated the politics and economics of the nation for so long. It also established psychological, as well as economic, opposition to regulations affecting the use of privately owned land. During the nineteenth century, too, land speculation was rampant and generally accepted. It, too, became entrenched in the mores and institutions of the nation. When we speak of land policy and control today we are dealing with the commodity which, in the century before this one, afforded several million people economic opportunity, facilitated home ownership for hundreds of thousands who had never known it before, and became the basis for not a few fortunes. [17]

So the descendants of those people, instead of having a precedent for leaseholds as in England, have precedents against leaseholds and favoring speculation in land. Of course, as we became more urbanized, land policies were modified. There is a tradition of using eminent domain to acquire land for public purposes, and zoning was established during the second decade of the twentieth century. Slowly, but surely, we are moving toward comprehensive planning requirements in many federal aid programs. But further progress in land use and public policy will depend, in my opinion, more upon state than federal action.[18]

There is little consensus about the desirability of reducing the population of our large cities. Rather, apprehension is frequently expressed concerning their continuing loss of population. And even the most avid proponent of suburban living would hardly dare suggest governmental action to move industry out of them or reduce the volume of employment in them. Rather we have great concern for preserving and expanding the tax base of our central cities. Retention of industry and commerce is a principal means of doing this.

Therefore, whatever the primary role of new communities may be in this nation, it is certainly not to accomplish the stated objectives of the British new towns.

Despite the many similarities with the English in language and culture, our form of government differs greatly from theirs. For this discussion, the most significant difference is that their national government exerts much greater power over local governments than our national government exerts. It is interesting, for example, that new towns in Great Britain are a responsibility of the Ministry of Housing and Local Government. In this country, a 1962 proposal for a Department of Urban Affairs was attacked, in part, because the name conjured up an erroneous concept of national control over local government. Thus the possibility that our national government will establish and carry out a direct program of planning and building new communities is slight. Also, our tax structure, with such great reliance of the local government upon real estate taxes, reinforces opposition to reduction of employment in, or dislocation of industry from, central cities.

In light of these circumstances, it should be apparent that new communities in the United States will differ from new towns in England.

No pattern of living yet devised by man is either perfect or without its detractors. The new towns I have visited in Great Britain are generally impressive in site planning but frequently pedestrian in housing design. Many observers agree that the most visually delightful of European new towns is Tapiola in Helsinki, Finland—a private nonprofit development which, in many respects, is more similar to the new communities of America than the new towns of Europe. But in this lovely setting of good site planning and excellent architecture, the unskilled workers find few accommodations and the construction costs are alarmingly high.

I have been slightly disturbed, also, by the adverse comments I have encountered from residents in England and elsewhere relative to the dullness of life in new towns. Already, a body of literature critical of them is developing.[19]

None of this is really damning. There is every reason to suspect that the architecture of English new towns is more a reflection of British attitudes than a characteristic of new towns *per se*. And no doubt the pressure of getting construction quickly under way after the war was also a factor. The social shortcomings may well reflect youth and growing pains. No doubt they were due, in part, to the adverse reaction of people who were attracted to them largely because of employment opportunities rather than in response to the housing environment they afforded. There is evidence, too, that a part of "new town blues" stems from the failure to provide the necessary basic core of commercial, recreational, and cultural facilities from the start. Real merit resides in this quotation from the 1960 annual report of the Ministry of Housing and Local Government: "The malady known as 'new town blues' has been greatly exaggerated in some press articles, but it undoubtedly exists. Social workers and doctors have long recognised it as one of the difficulties . . . which perhaps only time can overcome."[20]

NEW COMMUNITIES IN AMERICA

It is highly unlikely that a large number of American counterparts of European self-contained new towns will soon appear. New communities in this country will be conceived, planned, and constructed primarily by private developers.[21] Thus they will not be a revival of the

Greenbelt developments of the New Deal era, which were the first publicly developed American garden cities in the tradition of Ebenezer Howard. They will not be replicas of Britain's new towns. Rather, many will be descendants of Park Forest in Illinois. Here private developers, with an unprecedented support from the federal government, effected certain significant economies in land utilization, and stressed the need for adequate public facilities at the outset. This new community pioneered in the cluster development concept—a grouping of houses compactly but adjacent to considerable open space.* Thus in the initial program of more than 3,000 garden apartments, almost 90 percent of the land area in the apartment program was made available for common use, including a generous amount of landscaped open space. Also, significant savings, permitting reasonable rents, were made in the cost of utility lines and the street network.[22]

Park Forest, some thirty miles from Chicago, was the first American new-community development started and finished during the immediate post-World War II period. It demonstrated that American private enterprise is capable of creating novel and advanced patterns of urban

---

* "In cluster developments there is private land, which includes the house plots, and common land, from which all the houses benefit. The common land is often a community 'green,' in the tradition of the New England village. The green can be park or woods, or a cooperative recreation area like a golf course or swimming pool . . . The result is better-sited, better-looking, more interesting kinds of houses, more open, unspoiled land saved from the bulldozer and a more 'natural' environment." Ada Louise Huxtable, "'Clusters' instead of 'Slurbs,'" *New York Times Magazine*, Feb. 9, 1964, pp. 40, 42.

living. And, perhaps more important, it proved that such development was economically feasible.

In the years ahead we will see a great diversity of increasingly large developments in this nation. We are already familiar with the Levittowns which, though less imaginative and exciting than Park Forest, achieved economies through mass construction and land development techniques in large-scale subdivisions, including swimming pools and self-contained neighborhood facilities. Recently it has been reported that William B. Levitt has upgraded his planning, that he is emphasizing curving streets and minimizing use of the bulldozer so as to preserve trees and the other natural attributes of suburban sites.[23] But his are not new communities in the sense that the term is used by me.

Other and broader concepts of metropolitan community development are being initiated. Reston, a new community in Fairfax County, Virginia, located near Dulles International Airport and eighteen miles from Washington, is under construction. It represents a significant achievement in large-scale land assembly. Over 40 percent of the ten square miles to be developed will remain in open space, principally parks and recreation land. With high standards of design, architectural diversity, and good site planning, this new community is expected ultimately to have 75,000 residents. It will provide single standing homes, town houses, and apartment buildings of wide varieties, yet reflecting imaginative design. Builders of individual homes, small and large builders, as well as the sponsors, will be involved in the construction program. Reston will include bridle paths, stables, golf courses, tennis courts, and artificial lakes. Many types of commercial, educational, and cultural facilities will be provided. The sponsors also hope to have government office buildings and a variety of industrial development.[24]

The new community of Columbia in Howard County, Maryland, will contain 15,000 acres lying between Baltimore and Washington. In planning it, the sponsor is seeking new and exciting concepts for the total development of a new suburban city. According to the plan, a high level of industrial employment opportunities and commercial development will afford the variety and vitality that render urban life interesting and satisfying. A degree of ethnic and economic class diversification is also contemplated. Columbia's developer is working with new concepts in transportation, recreation, and education. Of course, he, too, is encouraging new and advanced architectural design, and he is paying special attention to land utilization.[25]

Both Reston and Columbia will provide a new type of living, aesthetically attractive, affording economies in land use, and assuring provision of utilities and other public facilities of high quality. Both Reston and Columbia are being developed around a town center. They avoid the British defect of failing to provide adequate community facilities during the earlier stages of development. Each of these communities is conceived of as a single organized system which brings together a number of new villages, a feature which may or may not contribute to their social and economic viability.

New communities facilitate well-planned, large-scale development. Thus they represent a potential beneficial long-term investment in the utilization of our land resources. And they can exert a deflationary influence upon land values. This would follow because less reliance would be placed upon utilization of land now held for speculation. New communities are usually farther removed from urban centers than land held for speculation and thus are on cheaper land. Their greatest economic impact results from their augmenting the supply of residential land in large increments.

Private sponsors of new communities are able to achieve high standards of development, with variety and mixture in housing design, that are impossible in the incremental, haphazard development of smaller-scale subdivisions. They are also in a position to influence positively local regulations affecting land use and building methods. Thus, new communities can provide a significant laboratory for demonstrating how zoning, subdivision controls, and building codes can be improved. For instance, zoning might be used to retard rather than accelerate inflation in land costs. Similarly, building codes could be based on more realistic performance standards than now generally exist. The well-financed developer, too, has the scope to develop and implement new standards for architectural control. Indeed, there may be real design premiums incident to private finance since this type of financing "has the advantage of insuring that the design . . . is closely attuned to the needs of the public." [26] Our better privately financed new communities will, I believe, have more architectural character and more attractively designed houses than the British new towns.

New communities can provide a setting for experimentation and innovation in many other fields. In them more efficient and effective institutions for education, recreation, communications, and transportation could be established. Instead of adjusting these activities to an existing physical environment and an established complex system of governmental restrictions (as we are forced to do to varying degrees in the existing urban areas), it will be possible to determine first what man's requirements are and then create a physical environment responsive to these needs.

THE ROLE OF NEW COMMUNITIES IN SUBURBIA

Clearly, new communities are desirable and possible in this country. In the United States we shall probably develop some new communities which are an integral part of the metropolitan areas. Most will be far removed from central cities. Both groups will frequently contain many of the desirable elements of the city. Here, as in Europe, the new communities will be large-scale developments, providing thousands of residential units. Included, in varying mixes, will often be libraries, parks, theaters, and shops. Some will have offices, factories, and industries that afford opportunities for work close at hand. Unlike the European new towns, the residents in our new communities will not generally walk or ride a bicycle to work; here the more common mode of transportation will be the automobile, as it seems to be becoming in Europe. However, in proportion as employment opportunities are nearby, the necessity for commuting will be reduced. Moreover, new communities represent orderly growth, a most favorable condition for the development and extension of mass transportation facilities linking central city, traditional suburbs, and new communities.

Of course, there will be many phony new communities in America. As the concept gains acceptance and catches the imagination of our people, there will be a tendency to identify any large subdivision as a new community. Some alleged to be new communities will be better-laid-out suburbs, but devoid of adequate community facilities, cultural and recreational institutions, and employment opportunities.

There is a role for government in the encouragement and development of new communities. It can be effected through financial assistance to local public agencies which elect to sponsor and assist in the assembly and improvement of land for such communities. But one must recognize that, at present, there are few such local public agencies able, willing, and ready to perform these functions. Thus primary reliance must be placed upon working through the increasing number of private investors and sponsors who are prepared to enter the field of well-planned, large-scale housing developments.

The new communities which will increasingly appear in this country will not solve our problems of future suburban development. As a matter of fact, most of this growth in the years immediately ahead will not occur in new communities: it will continue to be accommodated in smaller, more conventional subdivisions. We must, therefore, be concerned with the quality of these developments, encouraging conformity with a metropolitan plan, insisting that there be adequate provision of basic facilities such as water, sewers, and open spaces. In addition there must be encouragement of better land use which preserves trees and contours. Obviously, government at all its levels has a key responsibility for achieving these results.

There are signs that the home-building industry is recognizing the necessity for planning, designing, and building homes for the complete environment of the homeowner. In December 1964 the National Association of Home Builders in its annual convention issued a policy statement spelling out such an objective. "Our American society," the resolution affirmed, "is increasingly oriented to the home as the center of the American environment. The whole complex of environmental factors—cultural and physical—require intensive examination. To that end, we have commenced and intend to continue to study the relationship of the design and construction of homes to man's aesthetic, physical, and sociological environment."

Despite the concern of home-builders for better-planned and executed suburban developments, most of their efforts will be concentrated upon producing what will primarily be conventional subdivisions. And even the new communities which are now in planning and execution will not realize the full potential of this form of development. Though the hundred-odd existing and projected American new communities represent feasible examples of an extremely attractive style of life for the middle-income and upper-income family, the broad base of our economic pyramid—more than a third of the total population—is usually excluded.[27] This is the element in our society which is necessary for the successful operation of industrial and commercial facilities, as well as for manning the multiplicity of local services, such as janitorial, domestic, and retail services, and maintenance work. For new communities which are remote from concentrations of this manpower and womanpower, the lack of such workers can be both inconvenient and uneconomic.

Our new communities, therefore, will face three alternatives: (1) to plan for the inclusion of housing for this essential component; (2) to occasion the development of unplanned shack towns nearby which will soon evolve into rural slums; or (3) to depend upon commuters to supply these labor requirements, with consequent high incidence of absenteeism and upward pressures on labor costs. The higher labor costs, in large measure, would reflect high transportation costs and inconveniences.

Although I am a firm and long-time advocate of open occupancy and economic diversification in housing and have repeatedly emphasized the importance of such patterns in suburbia, I cannot delude myself into the belief that new communities will be a principal or the exclusive means of achieving these objectives. As in other respects, they can provide demonstrations of what can be done, but the quantitative impact will be slight. For one thing, the new communities will not be numerous enough. For another, many private sponsors of new communities are sufficiently affluent to obtain financing from conventional sources which are not subject to federal standards.

Nevertheless, everything possible should be done to encourage the new communities to choose the first of their three alternatives—that is, to include housing for low-income residents along with higher-income groups. We need direct inducements to outlying communities to welcome the less affluent; financial assistance to make it possible for private developers to build for them (with adequate safeguards written in the law); and wider coverage and effective enforcement of the Executive Order on Equal Opportunity in Housing. This order, issued by President Kennedy in November 1962, prohibits racial discrimination in certain types of publicly assisted housing.

Proponents of new towns in the United States frequently tend to exaggerate the degree of diversification in European new towns. In addition, such diversification as exists is hardly a unique attribute of those towns; rather it is due to the European tradition of including many economic classes in publicly assisted housing. Indeed, my impression is that class diversification is significantly less characteristic of European new towns than in other types of subsidized housing. The significance of new communities in this regard could, however, be much greater in the United States. For here the need is to break an entrenched suburban tradition of economic and racial homogeneity, and this can best be accomplished in a large new development.

Logically, restriction of government financial assistance in suburbia to new communities that meet certain requirements of economic diversity, planning, and open occupancy would encourage a suburban environment which would satisfy the objectives of many critics of existing suburbs. A leading proponent of such action advocates creation of new communities pursuant to regional open-space and transportation plans, and says, "These towns will also accommodate industrial workers and industries displaced [from the central cities]." [28] They would be open to nonwhites as well as whites, thereby serving as the instrument for breaking down ethnic ghettos in suburbia.

But legislation limiting federal assistance to new communities and excluding more conventional subdivisions will not be enacted in the near future. Thus, our challenge for the present is to extract the maximum from new communities and influence, as far as possible, the nature of the other suburbs of tomorrow, at the same time that we utilize the public lands placed in urban use, making them a symbol of national policy.

In the next chapter, I shall discuss urban renewal, indicating that many of its current problems stem from the confusion as to its objectives and from its earlier tendency to promise too much. Much of the sound criticism of the program is in the form of accusations that it has not produced what it was expected to achieve or what its proponents said it would. Actually these goals and claims were so broad—and often so inconsistent —that only a miracle could have fulfilled them. There is a similar danger that the champions of new communities in this country may damage their cause by claiming too much for the program.

There seems to be some appreciation of this danger. Wolf Von Eckhardt, architectural writer and critic, has presented a relatively balanced analysis of the role of new communities, saying: "New towns far out from the city are not the only answer. But we can no longer afford to build just housing. We must build communities or transform existing 'projects' into communities. Communities worthy of the name are first of all a matter of comprehensive design—not of social policy alone, or economics alone, planning alone or architecture alone, but a vigorously creative combination of all of this. The primary need of the Great Society is not just to build new towns but to build an environment in which a civilization can grow." [29]

Such an environment takes time to create. It has to be formulated and described, and in a democracy it must achieve widespread support. It is unfortunate that the dialogue about these matters did not start earlier, and that it has engaged so few persons. The population explosion which will occasion another rash of suburban expansion is upon us. It is, no doubt, comforting to cite England's experience and suggest our taking it over, lock-stock-and-barrel. To me this is not only unwise but improbable.

A few successes will do more to secure the popular

support needed to push the program than anything else. If Columbia and Reston achieve what their sponsors envision and if the people of this nation respond to what they offer, the dialogue will have passed from the theoretical to the practical.

One large-scale new development, Crofton, Maryland, has elicited favorable consumer response. Among its attributes which seem to attract the public are features which reflect careful community planning and enlightened land use. First there is the Village Green, inspired by the small shops at Williamsburg, including a tavern completely decorated in eighteenth-century style and open for business. In addition, attention has been paid to landscaping. For this, too, the sponsor made significant investments: "He put all the utilities underground, he saved every possible tree, even making islands in his parking lots to preserve trees. He landscaped entrance roads, his main boulevard and public areas and he bought thousands of yards of the best sod he could find. Everywhere there is a feeling of open space—at the entrances, around the Village Green and the acres of wooded parks that surround the recreation club and in the long vistas to be seen on and around the golf course." [30]

New communities are not the only pattern for the suburban sector of the urban complex. The late Catherine Bauer Wurster discussed the functions and structure of urban areas and asked these pertinent questions: "Do the pieces [which make up the urban complex] fit together only at the metropolitan level no matter what its size, or are there limitations of scale for certain everyday urban

functions? Is the implicit assumption of most metropolitan transportation plans substantiated—that the metropolis is essentially a single diversified market for housing,
jobs and leisure-time facilities? Or is relatively balanced
and integrated development feasible or desirable within
metropolitan subareas? This is the premise behind proposals for New Towns or relatively self-sufficient satellite communities, and for more housing in the central
city suited to the tastes and resources of middle- and
upper-income people who work there." Mrs. Wurster
characterized the new-towns concept as an old reform
movement: "Rather scorned by the current *avant-garde*,
it is quite as much an urbanist, anti-sprawl philosophy as
it is anti-Big City." [31]

It must be recognized that for us to accept new communities as the form of future urban expansion, our people would have to replace their apparent current desire
for private space with a greater concern for accessibility,
diversity, and other traditional urban values. But those
values are just what most people who have moved to the
suburbs seem to have abandoned. Who, then, are the
constituency which will press for new communities now?
But if this form of land utilization is placed in proper
perspective—as an important element in a rational approach to future suburbia—we can create effective public
opinion to press for an effective urban land policy.

To add to our uncertainty, it must be observed that
some countries have recently combined different types of
form and structure for their urban complexes. Sweden,
for example, has developed new towns, but it has mixed

them with a movement for pulling the metropolis together into a single city. In Vallingby, industry did not develop as rapidly as expected and this new town is largely a satellite of Stockholm. Also, this statement relative to Vallingby is pertinent: "It isn't easy for all the members of a family to find suitable work in their own part of town, and even if it should chance to succeed, the opportunity of changing employment arises more often than the opportunity of changing homes." [32] If this be true in Sweden, the first part of it is much more significant in the United States, suggesting that we shall not develop many self-contained new communities in the near future.

This is not, as some who oppose additional federal assistance for suburban development suggest, a basis for delay or denial of federal support for new communities in the United States. Many of those who oppose such action are fearful that it will decrease the amount of federal financial assistance for the central city. The Housing and Urban Development Bill of 1965 negates such an appraisal. Not only did the administration propose support of new communities, but it also proposed expanded types of, and augmented funds for, federal assistance to central cities. Included were grants for neighborhood community facilities, a new program of open-space grants in congested areas, and grants for beautification in central cities. (These proposals are described in greater detail in subsequent chapters). In addition, the urban renewal program was expanded and modified. These modifications were designed, in part, to increase the capacity of central cities to absorb a larger program.

At this time, when we are just beginning to produce new communities, it is imperative that there be some demonstrations of the feasibility of housing low-income, moderate-income, and high-income families in well-designed and attractive communities which excite people's imagination and promise to afford a new form of suburban living. Without federal assistance and federal standards few, if any, will emerge.

Actually the central cities have much to gain from this type of suburban development. It would envision the urban area as a totality. This, in turn, would encourage area-wide concern for the location of industrial, commercial, and housing facilities. The role of the central city as part of the urban complex could (and should) be a factor in determining the functions and institutions of the new communities. In such suburban development there could also be a realistic appraisal of the functions of both the central city and the new community. Based upon such an analysis we could start developing viable urban complexes which would better serve man's needs. Since new solutions to these needs would probably be more easily effected in newly created rather than existing communities, the central city would be in a position to adapt innovations which it could never pioneer within its own boundaries.

Thus, federal support for new communities is not an anti-central-city proposal. Rather it is an indispensable element in an area-wide approach to land utilization and urban development. Such an approach must, if it is to succeed, coordinate and reconcile the needs and functions of all elements which constitute the urban complex. New communities, planned in the context of area-wide considerations, can make a significant contribution to rational expansion of urban development. This expansion, in turn, will strengthen the central city and delineate more clearly its role in urban America.

But this does not require or suggest that all suburban expansion immediately or ultimately be in the form of new communities. Since, after all, we are a pragmatic people, I am convinced that before there can, or will, be a public acceptance or a public policy of adopting the new communities as *the* form, as contrasted to *a* form, of future suburban development, we will have to be surer than we now are that these communities will work. It is my guess that this form of suburban living will have an immediate appeal for a segment of the population. As it takes form and is observed, described, and discussed, the numbers attracted to it will increase. Simultaneously, others will find new communities deficient in many regards. No doubt, serious defects will develop.

The suburbia which is frequently criticized today takes a form which, though not articulated in public policy, was *de facto* public policy because of federal income tax provisions and mortgage-insurance support by the Federal Housing Administration. And some of us will recall that this kind of suburbia created at least as many problems as it solved; included, of course, was encouragement of exodus from the central city. Most of those problems were unanticipated. Will not the electorate ask if similar by-products are inherent in the new-community approach? Will not overemphasis upon new communities militate against effective concern and action for better suburban development in the future?

I am concerned, not only with a decade or so ahead, but with the remainder of this decade and the years immediately following. By 1970 we shall be at a level of two million housing starts a year. It is of crucial importance that the houses we then produce and those we build in the intervening years not have septic tanks that are wet and wells that are dry. We must act now to discourage the bulldozing away of contours and trees. We should improve the flow of traffic through encouraging, revitalizing, and initiating mass transportation. We need to act now to discourage culturally sterile suburban housing developments devoid of, or deficient in, shops, theaters, libraries, and parks within easy access. Nor can we afford to countenance continuing scatteration and uneconomic utilization of urban land.

In a word, we must take immediate action to create better suburbs and to provide an urban setting which increasingly recognizes the need for metropolitan planning. But, alas, there is no magic in planning. As a process *per se* it has little significance even when it operates in the context of clearly established goals, adequate factual materials, and efficient professional guidance, unless there is widespread citizen participation, as well as local political involvement. Only then can planning provide a vehicle for achieving a rational urban environment.

Neither urban planning nor its distortion is new. Very

recently, a group of archeologists discovered, in Turkey, the remains of a city believed to be over 8,000 years old. Moreover, they uncovered evidence of a city plan, with houses and markets carefully laid out in ordered pattern. This is believed to be the oldest executed city plan in existence. But those who dwelt in the orderly arrangement it facilitated did not seem to have been concerned primarily with the good life. Instead, according to John Melleart, assistant director of the British Institute of Archeology, they appear to have been preoccupied with fertility and death.[33]

I do not mean to imply that such preoccupations might be supposed to provide the basis for city planning, although we are certainly much occupied by fertility, and unless we plan more carefully we are in danger of killing our chances for decent living. What I am saying is that fertility—our great growth—should not be viewed as a death sentence for our great cities or their metropolitan fringes. Rather, in my view, this growth offers unparalleled opportunity to achieve a standard and scale of living no society has yet been able to devise. It all depends on how we utilize our urban land, the degree to which we harness our technology and affluence to provide more attractive and viable communities, and the extent to which we foster the development of opportunity and choice for all.

3

URBAN RENEWAL

URBAN RENEWAL was conceived in controversy and it has matured in controversy. In the process, two extreme schools of thought have grown up. On the one hand, there are those who can see no good in the program and would do away with it. The champions of urban renewal have often been equally dogmatic in its defense, denouncing all critics as biased and all criticisms as unfair.

The most extreme expression of the first point of view is found in Martin Anderson's *The Federal Bulldozer*, published in 1964. My principal criticism of this analysis is that it presented data which were from two to three years old (in describing a program started some fifteen years ago) and constantly asserted that they reflected a current situation. Actually great changes were made in urban renewal after 1961 and 1962. There are many detailed distortions in the book, but they represent program performance evaluations and have no place in this discussion.[1] Almost simultaneously with the appearance of Mr. Anderson's book, an analysis of the relocation of persons displaced by urban renewal projects was published by a doctoral fellow at the Joint Center for Urban

Studies of M.I.T. and Harvard. It, too, used outdated data to justify a current evaluation and, although the author cited post-1960 reports, he failed to indicate in his text that the recent data reflected a significant improvement in the relocation process.[2]

Finally, James Q. Wilson, Director of the Joint Center for Urban Studies of M.I.T. and Harvard, in an article entitled "Urban Renewal Does Not Always Renew," has advised us that "there is no 'urban problem' in the United States today except, perhaps, for the problem of urban aesthetics." He goes on to explain that he means there are "no problems of cities *per se*," and that it seems to him the housing problem "is also a fiction, or very nearly so." Mr. Wilson writes, "When I say there is no urban problem and no housing problem, this does not mean that we do not have problems in the cities. But they are not problems of the cities themselves, and they are not problems of the housing in those cities. They are the problems of the people in those cities. We have three major problems in our cities: a poverty problem, a race problem, and a cultural problem . . . I mean culture . . . in an anthropological and not in a high-brow sense."[3] If one took Mr. Wilson's original statement literally, one might well ask why, then, is there a center for the study of a problem that does not exist?

These dicta about urban and housing problems, even when put in context, become the basis for an all-out attack upon federal programs for urban renewal and related activities. In the opinion of the *Wall Street Journal*, "such refreshing heresy should be heeded in Washington as Congress considers President Johnson's new housing program." [4] Of course, urban and housing problems have human and aesthetic aspects; they also have physical manifestations, two of the most important of which are the economic health of urban areas and the quality of housing. And Mr. Wilson recognizes this, as was evidenced by his support of President Johnson's Housing and Urban Development Bill in April 1965. However, by issuing dramatic statements—which are of dubious validity—he became an authority cited in opposition to the very legislation for which he subsequently testified. [5]

Concurrently the defenders of the urban renewal program have frequently become extremely defensive. As a consequence of such hardened attitudes on the part of both the critics and the defenders, much of the current literature on urban renewal is in terms of absolutes. It is time we developed more objective and reasoned anlaysis.

In this war of words, and often invective, there is much lost effort in that the proponents and the opponents frequently fail to establish a common definition of the program's objectives. Urban renewal suggests quite different goals to different people. [6]

As I indicated in the preceding chapter, one of the difficulties lies in the fact that the earlier champions of the program claimed too much for it. Thus, it was inevitable that the critics would disclose failures to produce what had been set forth as the potential benefits.

Of course, there is also much controversy as to what actually happened. This involves the challenging of data, the selection and interpretation of data, and the evaluation of day-to-day administration of the program. In this chapter I shall avoid such controversy save for an analysis of the relocation process.[7] Rather, my concern will be to set forth the nature of urban renewal and attempt to formulate its current objectives. When this is done there is a sounder basis upon which to evaluate both the program and the literature that relates to it.

Nathan Glazer, confirmed critic of urban renewal, has described the objectives in these terms:

"Urban Renewal is the program that was designed to clear the slums of the central city, by giving public agencies Federal subsidies and the power of eminent domain to condemn sites, to demolish buildings, and to resell the cleared tracts to those who would build on them in accordance with a general plan that would improve the city. The objectives were to reduce substandard housing; to replace it with better housing; to retain in the central city middle-class white families tempted to move away, or to pull them back from the suburbs if they had already moved; to strengthen the tax base of the central cities, threatened by this loss of wealthier citizens, so that the cities could provide better education and social services. Above these specific objectives was a larger one: the realization of the good city . . ." [8]

This is an adequate description of the announced objectives of urban renewal. Its author evaluates the program's performance on the basis of these goals and —not surprisingly—finds deficiencies. But what most

disturbs Glazer and others is not really the performance in relation to the objectives of urban renewal he
has delineated but the objectives themselves, save the
amorphous one of realizing the good city. The issue
is whether or not a program of subsidies designed to
revitalize our cities is justified if in the course of its
operations it displaces the poor, the discriminated
against, and the small neighborhood businessman.
Glazer, as contrasted to Martin Anderson, believes that
the program could be utilized to serve the social purposes
he feels are required as a justification for public financial
assistance.[9]

What Glazer minimizes and Anderson, as well as a
host of others, refuses to recognize is that urban renewal
has been modified during the last few years and that
current federal policy will modify it further.* Professor

* "Concentrating on the 1949–1962 period, Anderson disregards the
definite policy changes initiated by the Housing and Home Finance
Agency during the last few years. Relocation is being handled more
effectively today; there is greater sensitivity to the social problems
that accompany renewal; a new and potentially effective government
middle-income housing program has been introduced; and more
imaginative experiments are under way to provide publicly subsidized
housing for low-income families . . ." William W. Nash, Jr., and
Chester W. Hartman, "Laissez-Faire in the Slums," *The Reporter*,
Feb. 25, 1965, p. 49.

"Much of the criticism of urban renewal is based upon mistakes
made in the early years of the program, and urban renewal frequently
gets blamed for things outside its jurisdiction—such as property condemnation for construction of highways and other improvements.
This is not to say that urban renewal has achieved perfection, but
the program is making a commendable contribution toward better
urban living." This quotation is from "The Toil and Turmoil of
Urban Renewal," *Business Review* (Federal Reserve Bank of Philadelphia), January 1965, p. 19.

Wilson is a little more sophisticated. He admits that there have been recent changes in urban renewal, but then proceeds to cite Anderson's study which ignored the very changes Wilson has duly noted. On the basis of this study, Mr. Wilson arrives at evaluations and conclusions.[10]

But the program's earlier goals are not a durable set of objectives in a society which is concerned with an attack upon poverty and the achievement of the good life for all elements in the nation.

THE EVOLUTION OF URBAN RENEWAL

Urban renewal is not unique in being indefinite in its stated objectives. Indeed, it seems that all our efforts associated with slum clearance have been so characterized. The first major one was public housing, which got started through a clause in the National Industrial Recovery Act. It was mentioned as a type of public works and gained acceptance as an instrument for increasing employment. Subsequently the program was sold partly as public works, partly as slum clearance, and partly as low-income housing. This confusion persisted, finding expression, for example, in the legislative requirement for equivalent demolition of slums whenever vacant sites were utilized.

Urban renewal has followed in this tradition, but with the additional difficulty that some of its objectives conflict with others.

The first controversy incident to urban renewal was over the form of the subsidy. Soon that gave way to differences of opinion relative to the degree to which urban redevelopment should be concerned with shelter. The issue had to do with the relative importance of housing, slum clearance, and redevelopment. Also, of course, this ultimately led to differences over the type of redevelopment—the mix between residential, commercial or industrial, and public construction. Within the universe of residential construction there were differences over the economic classes that should be housed.

As the program matured, these issues continued to harass it. They are still unsolved and, in my opinion, occasion much of the confusion which adheres to urban renewal. Today, discussion of them is complicated by other issues and objectives which are articulated by those who operate and evaluate the program. Until there is some consensus about the basic objectives and possible achievements of urban renewal, it will continue to be surrounded by confusion.

The principal early advocates of an urban redevelopment program were organizations such as the Urban Land Institute and the American Institute of Planners. Their basic concern was with the physical and economic development of the entire urban area. As early as 1945, Alfred Bettman of the American Institute of Planners set forth the position in his testimony before the Taft Subcommittee on Housing and Urban Redevelopment. Slums were treated as but one important phase of urban blight, and housing as but one form of redevelopment. Urban redevelopment, in the opinion of these organizations, could not be considered as merely housing or housing with minor variations. Redevelopment should be applied to all urban areas which needed it and would include all classes of land use.[11]

There was, also, a strong economic argument for this type of urban redevelopment. In 1941 it was set forth in an article by Guy Greer and Alvin H. Hansen, who outlined the problem to which urban renewal should be addressed, noted that, "with few exceptions, our American cities and towns have drifted into a situation, both physically and financially, that is becoming intolerable. Their plight, however, is getting worse."[12]

This emphasis upon the physical and financial, and the assignment of housing to a secondary place in the redevelopment process, were rejected by Senator Robert A. Taft. In 1945 he was joined by other members of the Subcommittee on Housing and Urban Redevelopment of the Senate Special Committee on Post-war Economic Policy and Planning in believing that all redevelopment projects should stress housing. His subcommittee recommended that any urban redevelopment program contain a "predominantly residential" requirement and that the federal government should not "embark upon a general program of aid to cities looking to their rebuilding in more attractive and economical patterns."[13] Later the Senate Committee on Banking and Currency similarly, and categorically, set forth the position that redevelopment should be limited to areas which are predominantly residential or scheduled primarily for residential re-use. "This limitation," the committee observed, "is fully justified in view of the fact that the primary purpose of

Federal aid in this field is to help remove the impact of slums on human lives rather than simply to assist in the redevelopment or rebuilding of cities." [14]

The proponents of nonresidential redevelopment did not give up easily. Instead they continued to press their position, achieving their first success in 1954 when a provision was enacted permitting up to 10 percent of federal grant funds to be used for projects not meeting the "predominantly residential" requirement. In 1959 the percentage was doubled and in 1961 was increased another 10 percent. Today the exemption is still 30 percent. The report of the Senate Committee on Banking and Currency on the Housing Act of 1961 indicates a real change in philosophy within that body: "With growing attention to the needs for downtown renewal, it appears necessary to increase the exception to provide for a greater number of projects of this type. The economic, institutional, and cultural bases of community life are increasingly recognized as necessary to the creation and continuing existence of good homes in sound urban neighborhoods." [15]

This new position by no means represents a complete abandonment of Congressional emphasis upon residential re-use in urban redevelopment. Two recent events demonstrate this. Both houses of Congress refused to enact an administration proposal for a further exemption up to 35 percent in 1964. And in the discussion of this matter, the current chairman of the Housing Subcommittee of the Senate Banking and Currency Committee, Senator John J. Sparkman, strongly set forth his conviction that the image and the emphasis of urban renewal should be on housing.

Meanwhile others, now primarily the local directors of urban renewal programs, pushed, and are pushing, for more downtown (i.e., predominantly *nonresidential*) redevelopment. The reasons for their position include the ideological concepts set forth by planners and economists a decade and a half ago and the significance of non-residential redevelopment for restoring downtown business; but practical, operational considerations are involved as well. The downtown redevelopment is dramatic; it is often more quickly put into execution than a comparable predominantly residential re-use; it usually provides high tax returns to the city; it reduces controversies over the income group to be served by residential re-use; and it is instrumental in attracting support from the business and financial power structure.

A TOOL FOR PRESERVING THE ECONOMIC HEALTH OF CITIES

One of the most persistent issues coming out of the conflict over the emphasis and direction of urban renewal relates to the tax benefits which urban renewal generates for local government. Actually the problem is more than a matter of taxes. It relates to the total economic health of the city. A major element in the decline of central cities is the erosion of their economic base. This may entail both a loss of sources of employment and a diminution of the real estate tax base. The solution of both of these problems is the principal objective of most proponents of downtown renewal, which can, and increasingly does, serve either to prevent the loss of businesses or to attract new businesses to the core areas of our cities.* Constitution Plaza in Hartford, Gateway Center in Minneapolis, Church Street Redevelopment in New Haven, and Charles Center in Baltimore, to mention only a few, are successful examples of this. In each instance not only was employment and business retained and expanded but real estate taxes were appreciably increased.[16]

The true issue is not residential versus nonresidential, nor downtown renewal versus renewal in the deteriorating "gray areas" between the core and the more affluent fringes, but the proper combination of these elements in a local redevelopment program. Cities are composed, first, of people, and the proper housing of the residents is important. But cities also have to have an economic base. The elements of the economic base have changed; today there is less of the heavy and dirty types of manufacturing, more light and clean industry, a growing amount of research, and a greater volume of commercial, cultural, and service activities. These require new types of offices, plants, stores, and public buildings. And they cannot be built on improved land in the central city as cheaply as they might be built on much less expensive vacant land on, or beyond, the fringe of the city. Thus, if the central city is to become economically healthy, it needs to provide space and facilities for those

---

* It should be noted that downtown renewal, though predominantly nonresidential, usually includes *some* housing and public buildings. The definition of a nonresidential redevelopment is one that is less than 51 percent residential.

economic activities which it can attract and hold. In addition to the cost factor, as basic as it is, there are other elements which influence the location of business activities. As far as industry is concerned, the availability of adequate space for the construction of horizontal rather than vertical plants is important. Also, the need for adequate parking space or the existence of efficient mass transportation are elements which determine where industry locates.[17]

Urban renewal provides needed ingredients. One is eminent domain, which puts the city in a position to acquire a total area and deal with it as a unit. Another is subsidies, which are even more basic, because there could be eminent domain without a federal subsidy program. The subsidies make it possible to provide cleared sites at marketable prices in central locations, and therefore accelerate and increase the demand for the use of such land. In addition urban renewal provides the major source of financing for redeveloping core areas with good traffic-flow patterns, pedestrian malls, adequate lighting, and other amenities which make downtown business, industrial, and commercial redevelopment competitive with similar facilities in the suburbs.

There remains a problem. Nonresidential redevelopment usually pays off for the city. It produces more tax revenue; so why shouldn't the locality pay back the federal contribution to it?[18] At the outset it must be recognized that, once the redevelopment has been completed, such repayment is mathematically possible. But is it desirable?

The reason the federal government is in the field of

urban renewal is that the cities do not have the financial resources to undertake it unassisted. Were cities to raise their own revenue for urban redevelopment, such action would involve higher local taxes, and this would accelerate the exodus of businesses and higher-income families. To avoid this acceleration of a vicious cycle of financial deterioration, the cities must seek financial aid elsewhere to help bring about urban redevelopment. We have slowly recognized that economic rehabilitation is a vital part of urban redevelopment. Thus, the downtown projects not only provide physical upgrading and employment and business expansion but also establish a long-term source of increasing taxes. If this tax flow is to have maximum impact, it should not be taken back by the federal government.

Somewhat related to downtown renewal is the argument over the type of residential redevelopment that is most desirable. This matter got off to a bad start because of the conviction of some of the early proponents of urban renewal that it would be a major instrument to cure the financial ills of our cities. Thus it was inevitable that they became the champions of housing which would provide the basis for higher real estate assessments. This sort of housing, when combined with nonresidential redevelopment, would, so they claimed, generate four to six dollars of private investment for each dollar of public expenditure,[19] and it would greatly augment the real estate tax take. Unfortunately there are limitations to the program's capacity to generate tax revenue. In the first place, the demand for high-rent housing in most central cities is thin (although it is sure to grow in the long run). In the second place, there developed an increasing public hostility to a program of federal subsidies which seems to take away from the poor and benefit the more affluent.

Of course, urban renewal, and especially subsidized downtown redevelopment, will distress the laissez-faire economist who will shout that it is public intervention and consequently uneconomic utilization of our resources. Certainly it is an effort to direct the location of certain activities to places other than where they would go if there were no governmental program. But there is sound economic justification for this. Our existing cities, for all their problems and deficiencies, contain an enormous amount of wealth, a great accumulation of public facilities, a large and varied inventory of housing. Most important, our cities have large populations, composed of men and women of many talents and specialized training. They have, too, complex organizations, administrative machinery, and facets of culture. Thus the issue is more than securing the most efficient arrangement of new productive resources. We also have to take into account the economic, social, and political losses incident to abandonment or decline of the existing resources, both human and physical.

Those laissez-faire economists who are consistent oppose *all* forms of public subsidies, including those like Federal Housing Administration mortgage insurance and federal subsidies for highways. Some condemn all aid to agriculture, young industries, and even the postal system. The fact is, however, that urban renewal was initiated at a time when there were subsidies to encourage exodus from the central city. Theoretically, such subsidies could have been phased out or abolished. Such action, however, seems unlikely and, even if taken, would not have reversed the spiral of central-city decay. To advocate such action is to accept the notion that our existing cities will and should die. This I reject.

Technological, as well as economic, issues are involved. As one writer puts it, "The taller buildings get, the costlier they are to tear down . . . To abandon existing cities, would be to scrap an investment estimated at over $500 billion . . . Much of that investment, of course, is still sound." [20] For it must be remembered that the city is a single, mammoth capital investment.

Victor Gruen has refuted the case for abandoning our cities in these words: "Even if, by some miracle, we could today write off all our existing cities like bad investments, it is highly doubtful that this would be a gain. We would be losing not only the best and most logical sites for urban developments, and enormous human and economic values, but we would also lose the continuity of human experience that makes life worthwhile. If we cannot muster the strength and ingenuity to reorganize and rebuild our existing cities, then I seriously doubt the availability of sufficient wisdom and ability to create new ones that will be any better." [21]

Mr. Gruen writes in the European tradition. On that continent cities are much older than ours and there is little advocacy of their abandonment. Rather they are valued institutions. One evidence of this which impressed me was the idea in France of using the old, and often abandoned, university cathedrals as the centers around which new towns would be developed. This is in contrast to the American dream of creating an urban environment anew[22]—a point of view which probably reflects our youth as a nation. It also expresses our values. "Urban renewal," says Lyle Schaller, "especially the recent emphasis on rehabilitation and conservation, also is in conflict with the frontier practices of American life. For decades Americans have been accustomed to discard the old, the used and the wornout and replace it with the new . . . The contemporary emphasis in urban renewal is in direct opposition to this good old American tradition."[23]

In England, as was set forth in the preceding chapter, new towns are designed, in part, to discourage further concentration of industry in existing cities. Thus they are self-contained and located far away from established centers of urban populations. The creation of an urban environment anew in that country is based upon an economic rationale and not a desire for newness *per se*. Nor is it assumed that existing cities are to be abandoned or permitted to wither away.

To permit our cities to die or continue to be weak and declining would be uneconomic and wasteful. Thus, action to retain certain economic functions in them is a sound investment and one which contributes to the better utilization of our resources.

The case for preserving and renewing our cities really

rests on what I consider the keystone of our national housing policy. It is concern for maximizing choices for the American people. As indicated in the preceding chapter, some of us prefer to live in a central city; others prefer to live in the suburbs. In order that these preferences may find realization, the central cities must be economically strong as well as attractive and functional. Urban renewal, though it cannot solve all the economic problems of our cities, is a tool to achieve these objectives, and crucial elements in its approach are revitalization of the downtown areas and provision of *some* higher-priced housing.

THE SLUMS AND THE DISLOCATION OF THE DISADVANTAGED

To the goal of strengthening the economic base is added another objective of urban renewal, somewhat related to the first, although in part conflicting. It is to strengthen the cultural base of the city. Involved are theaters, music halls, colleges and universities, schools, libraries, and museums. Many of these may support the economic base, but some are tax-exempt. Most of them would require affluent middle-class residents for support. One social benefit would flow from both these emphases: the clearance of slums. Simultaneously, however, a social cost occurred—dislocation of the poor and the discriminated against. It was to be offset by effective relocation; but this was slow to come about, and by now it is generally conceded that even with humane and effective relocation, enforced dislocation involves economic and psychological hardship.

Just as urban renewal will not and cannot solve all the economic and tax problems of our cities, neither can it be a cure-all for their housing ills. And this is hard for us to accept because there has been confusion on this score from the beginning of the effort. On the basis of earlier Congressional intent and the tradition of federal participation in housing and related problems, urban renewal was, and still is, looked at as primarily a slum clearance program which will ultimately eradicate all slums in American cities.[24] Two sophisticated and able students of, and practitioners in, the field published a pamphlet on urban renewal in Washington, D.C. under the title "No Slums in Ten Years." [25] Of course the ten years have passed and Washington still has slums. It also has a highly successful and attractive urban redevelopment which has pioneered in racial integration and replaces *one* of the worst slums in the nation's capital.[26]

Not only will urban renewal fail to clear all the slums, but I question if we shall ever rid our cities of them until we solve the economic, social, and psychological ills which harass modern man. It is, therefore, unfortunate that a single program, oriented principally to a segment of the physical aspects of housing, has become associated with a goal which is impossible for it to achieve. The sooner we divest ourselves of this romantic illusion, the better we will be able to assess our slum-clearance activities. Already this is being realized. Witness the emphasis upon rehabilitation of existing houses and upon code enforcement in recent housing legislation.

But the greatest romantic illusion in the discussions of

slums is not the hope that they will all be cleared in the near future, but the misconception that they are all stable neighborhoods to which the residents have strong ties.

The basis for this illusion is, in large measure, due to an earlier action of urban renewal—the demolition of the West End of Boston. This was, in many ways, an atypical blighted area, but it is the area most frequently studied in recent years.[27] Little of the analysis looks at the West End in an historical sense. It is my belief that the community was already an economic drain. The young people were moving out and Skid Row was fast encroaching. How long would it have held its stable population?

In the 1950's, however, it did have a population which, in large part because of age, had strong ties to the community and opposed moving away from it. But it requires no great sophistication to realize that what may have been found to exist (and this well may have been exaggerated once the residents were forced to move) among a group of elderly Boston Italians, who could have moved earlier into other neighborhoods but chose not to, was not typical of those who were displaced by urban renewal in its first decade of activity. For two thirds of these displaced persons were nonwhites who did not, and do not, enjoy a similar degree of mobility and therefore may have lived in a neighborhood not through attachment but because they had no choice.

A majority of both the whites and nonwhites who have left slums and blighted areas demolished by urban renewal were long-time residents of those areas. There are, however, significant geographical differences. In Northern communities, to which there has been vast nonwhite migration in recent decades, there are evidences of much greater stability of residence among whites than nonwhites. In the South, the nonwhites and whites in urban renewal areas are about the same in that respect; that is, about the same proportion have lived there a long time. Thus, nonwhites in Southern urban renewal areas have lived there considerably longer than nonwhites in Northern urban renewal areas.[28] This strongly suggests that in the North, slums occupied by whites have relative stability of occupancy but nonwhite slums seem to lack stability. And even where there is relative stability of occupancy in nonwhite slums, it usually reflects necessity rather than choice. Consequently, it is not necessarily an index of residents' attachment to neighborhoods but rather a reflection of restricted residential mobility which has long limited the housing choices of colored Americans.

The typical American urban slum is not necessarily a neighborhood which has great attractions for its occupants. Many of its residents evidence strong attachments to it only when they are faced with the prospect of being displaced without any certainty that they will be rehoused adequately elsewhere. If this were not so, the public housing program would have encountered much of the same neighborhood opposition that urban renewal has. Of course I recognize that in any slum there are those who are strongly attached to their neighborhood, and that there are some slums which are fairly cohesive communities. The point is that many occupants of slums are seeking to break out of them or are dissatisfied with the environment in which their incomes, race, or other factors force them to remain. Also, the turnover of residents, especially in Northern nonwhite slums, belies the concept of neighborhood stability.

As long as it was believed that we would be able to clear all of our slums through urban renewal, it was inevitable that questions of the timing and the cost of the undertaking would be raised. Thus, there are estimates of what the total effort would involve in dollars,[29] and there is advocacy of accelerating the program rapidly. Total slum clearance and total urban renewal became an alternative to which federal spending could be directed when and if our defense budget were materially reduced. This, too, is unrealistic. Urban renewal, involving slum clearance and dislocation, has a disruptive impact upon a locality, and there are economic, social, and political limitations upon the volume of it that can be digested in any period of time. We now are comprehending that urban renewal is not only a time-consuming operation but one that has to be paced to reflect the ability of cities to accommodate to its impact.

It is misleading, for example, to talk about the number of urban renewal projects that have been completed. Some, like the vast Southwest redevelopment in Washington, D.C., have been in execution for many years. By any reasonable standard, Southwest redevelopment is a success, but one reason for its success is that it was not prematurely completed. Because it transformed the nature of a large area, the timing of improvements was crucial. The phasing of the construction enabled the demand for the new fairly high-cost housing to grow as the supply increased. This housing is today renting briskly and the cooperative apartments and town houses are finding ready purchasers even before they are completed.

The other side of slum clearance is the provision of housing for low-income and moderate-income families. What has urban renewal done for these groups? What will it do for them?

Originally, the champions of urban renewal seem to have assumed that the low-income and moderate-income households would be able to upgrade their shelter through the filtering process. Thus, urban renewal sites would be developed primarily for higher-income families and the less affluent would go into the vacancies occasioned by a series of moves incident to new construction. In this process, it was assumed that all income groups could and would upgrade their housing. Of course, it did not work this way. The two major impediments were the general tightness of the housing market, which inhibited the assumed chain of vacancies, and the various frictions in the housing market, occasioned principally by racial bias and a paucity of good moderate-cost housing.[30]

Recently the housing market has changed. In most of the nation's cities there are sufficient vacancies to ease the process of relocation. This economic fact, when combined with much more stringent federal relocation requirements, has upgraded the rehousing of displaced households, albeit at rents which often have absorbed a somewhat higher proportion of income.

Perhaps even more important than the easing of the housing market has been the change in attitude toward relocation. At first it was considered no problem. Then it was ignored in some cities where poor families were pushed out of their homes with a minimum of assistance. Today most of those engaged in urban renewal are acutely conscious of the importance and difficulties of relocation, and this gives them greater concern for the ability of communities to adjust to the impact of the program. Federal legislation and federal policy recognize that relocation can and does entail economic costs and psychological stress among those who are forced to move.

Although I was at first resolved not to enter into an evaluation of the performance of urban renewal, no discussion of the program is meaningful if it ignores this aspect of relocation. Because of the earlier deficiencies in relocation, "conventional wisdom" has it that the situation, though somewhat better, is still deplorable. When the Housing and Home Finance Agency (HHFA) released data indicating that over three quarters of those relocated in the fiscal year ending June 1963 moved into decent, safe, and sanitary housing, those who view the program from academia responded that the figures were unreliable. They noted that the local public agencies which operate the program report the data and these agencies grossly overestimate progress. To prove their point, they cited a horror case. For they *know* that relocation is a scandal.[31]

I, too, have realized that there are questions relative to the accuracy of the locally reported data.[32] Therefore, I contracted with the U.S. Bureau of the Census to make a survey of families relocated during the period from June 1 to August 31, 1964. HHFA identified all local redevelopment agencies which had projects going into execution during 1962 and 1963 and where there had been relocation during the summer of 1964. The Census Bureau sample involved 132 cities containing about 60 percent of all those families relocated by urban renewal during the period of the survey.* During the three summer months of 1964, 2,842 families were relocated by urban renewal in the 132 localities; 2,300 of these were interviewed by the Bureau of the Census—the remainder had moved from the city, could not be located, or refused to respond. Of those interviewed, 94 percent had been relocated in standard housing.[33]

The firm recognition of the problems of dislocation is one of the forces behind the new directions of urban renewal, which will be described presently and which will be accompanied by housing programs designed to increase the amount of shelter for low-income and moderate-income families. Urban renewal cannot be evaluated in a vacuum. The Urban Renewal Administration is a part of the Housing and Home Finance Agency, where it is complemented by the activities of the Federal Housing Administration and the Public Housing Administration. In addition all HHFA programs are, in turn, a

---

* The remaining 40 percent were distributed widely among some 630 additional localities which had varying workloads of relocation. Most of these communities had small relocation programs incident to urban renewal.

part of the housing market upon which they act and to which they react.

It must be recognized, too, that there is no basis for the assumption that new living units should always be constructed in the same sites as the old ones or necessarily for the same occupants or income group. There are social and political reasons for minimizing the displacement of families by urban renewal or other actions, and when the poor are forced out by one program, other programs should compensate by providing more housing within their income capacity. But slum clearance is sure to bring some displacement.

If, as in urban renewal, this displacement occasions relocation from substandard to standard housing in eight out of ten cases, it is sure to involve some higher rentals. The striking and encouraging thing about the Census Bureau survey referred to above was that the degree of such increases was nominal.[34] The fact that these increases exist is the basis for the limited rent supplements for those displaced provided in the Housing and Urban Development Law of 1964 and the current proposals for much more comprehensive and long-term rent supplements for low-income and moderate-income families proposed in the 1965 bill.

NEW DIRECTIONS IN URBAN RENEWAL

Although urban renewal is a vital tool for preserving our cities, we must modify it in light of sound analyses and experience. Thus there have been, and there will continue to be, new directions in the program. Moderate-income housing and rehabilitation of existing housing will be stressed.

Both moderate-income housing, as a form of redevelopment, and rehabilitation, which is designed to minimize family displacement and economic dislodgment, were inspired by economic necessity as well as social policy and political expediency. Similarly, both were in conflict with the goal of building primarily for upper-middle-class families and maximizing the tax returns to the city.

Thus, urban renewal has had to reconcile and broaden its stated and imputed objectives, recognizing that it must be concerned with social as well as economic returns. In the process, its economic gains will be less than was at first anticipated. The objective must be to get as much economic impact as possible while occasioning the least degree of social costs and upgrading the living conditions of all elements in the population.

The recent redirections in the program and those suggested in President Johnson's message on "The Problems and Future of the Central City and Its Suburbs" (March 2, 1965) now offer a basis for redefining the functions of the program. They are as follows:

• Provide sites for new residential construction serving a variety of income groups. A limited amount of this will be higher-cost and serve to hold in, and attract to, central cities middle-class families. But most will be moderate-income and low-income housing.

• Continue to undertake downtown redevelopment. This will serve to strengthen the economic base of central cities. It will also make a contribution to increased tax revenue, but grants for social public facilities and for services will be a more direct and effective support to local government finance.

● Upgrade the quality of the existing supply of housing—especially in the dreary gray areas outside the central business districts—largely through new and expanded programs of rehabilitation and code enforcement.

● Demolish *some* of the dilapidated and substandard housing in the blighted areas.

● Afford sites for public institutions, particularly universities and hospitals.

● Provide sites for industrial redevelopment projects.

● Develop more attractive and better-planned cities.*

The volume of private expenditures and the amount of tax assistance to local government will be less than was previously contemplated, suggesting the need for other forms of revenue assistance to our cities. Hence the grants mentioned in the second point, above. To supplement indirect revenue assistance to cities via urban renewal, the federal government has proposed direct contributions. Included are the new program of matching

---

* The sequence of this list does not represent a system of priorities. In the first place, any one project or local program may well, and often does, perform several of these functions simultaneously. Secondly, in any city a project or a program may emphasize one or more of these objectives. It is imperative, therefore, that no system of inflexible priorities be established for urban renewal. However, as this analysis indicates, the main thrust of the program will be toward providing sites for residential redevelopment and rehabilitation and for revitalizing downtown areas. Urban renewal, of course, will involve slum clearance—either through demolition or rehabilitation—and it will serve to develop more attractive and better-planned cities.

grants for service facilities, such as neighborhood centers, and for acquisition of open spaces in congested neighborhoods. These will help cities carry out plans developed in connection with their community-action programs financed by the Economic Opportunity Act. In addition, federal funds are proposed to provide significant support for education, job training, and associated services.

These approaches recognize that cities need financial assistance to meet their required outlays for public facilities and services. They take the direct route and are more effective in assisting the provision of such facilities and services because they provide immediate financial relief without reducing tax revenue over the short run as urban renewal may well do.[35] Direct grants, however, are complementary to, and not a substitute for, urban renewal, which not only improves the local tax situation but supports the economic base of localities, upgrades the quality of housing, and serves to arrest blight and clear slums, at the same time that it encourages and facilitates orderly development of the localities. Direct grants can be, as they are, used primarily to assist the disadvantaged and the needy, providing services which are readily identified and politically accepted as those for which federal funds should be spent.

The goal of providing moderate-income housing in urban renewal areas is far from new. Apparently the early objective of urban renewal in many cities was to provide moderate-income housing on cleared sites. However, the existing tools of the federal government were inadequate for the task. An initial effort to meet the need was creation of Section 220 of the Federal Housing Act. This authorized the Federal Housing Administration (FHA) to provide mortgage insurance for residential developments in urban renewal areas and the purchase of such mortgages by the Federal National Mortgage Association (FNMA). The result was more and cheaper mortgage money for residential redevelopment; but moderate-income housing was not forthcoming. Thus, for the most part, even when, as in Chicago and Washington, the urban renewal plan specified moderate-income housing, it was impossible to produce it.

It was not until the Housing Act of 1961 was enacted that the situation improved. That legislation included still another new provision, Section 221(d)(3). This new provision authorized below-the-market-interest-rate mortgages, insured by FHA and purchased by FNMA. As a result, it was, for the first time, possible to construct moderate-income housing on a national scale.[36] Significantly, by the spring of 1965 the urban renewal projects in Chicago and Washington, referred to above, were in the process of adding a limited number of moderate-income housing to the large inventory of higher-priced accommodations already in occupancy.

Prior to 1961, New York State had had experience with a middle-income housing program for six years. This program was one which utilized low-interest, long-term mortgages financed by the state or localities. It was designed to serve income groups slightly higher than those encompassed by the Section 221(d)(3) program. (For a four-person family, median income under the New

York middle-income program was approximately $7,500; in the federal moderate-income program the figure was about $6,000.) And, until the federal moderate-income housing program became available, the middle-income housing program of New York was the only viable instrument to finance other than high-rent construction or public housing in urban redevelopment.

The impact of these two programs is reflected in recent statistics for urban redevelopment. As of June 1964, of the 61,777 residential units that had been completed in urban renewal sites, over 17 percent were developed under the middle-income program of New York State, 7.3 percent under the federal moderate-income program, and 8.5 percent for public housing. The remainder were for upper-income occupancy. On the vacant land conveyed or committed to a redeveloper in the fiscal year 1964, preliminary figures indicated that about 35 percent of the residential units would be developed under the federal moderate-income program, 9.4 percent under moderate-income sales' programs of the Federal Housing Administration, 6 percent under New York's middle-income program, 3 percent under the direct loan program for senior citizens, and 7.4 percent by public housing. Thus, whereas at the end of the fiscal year 1964 only one third of the residential units constructed in urban renewal areas were for lower-income occupancy, three fifths of the units scheduled for future development are planned for such occupancy.

Most critics of urban renewal have emphasized its failure to recognize the human ingredients in the activity.

The more objective among them also recognize the achievements of the program, but assert that it, like any slum clearance program, is vulnerable unless it is co-ordinated with, and facilitates, activity to augment the supply of housing available to groups displaced.[37] This indicates a major emphasis upon rehabilitation of the existing supply of housing, as one of the required tools.

But this rehabilitation must be cost-conscious—designed to accommodate approximately the same income groups as resided in the structures prior to their being improved. The Housing and Urban Development Bill of 1965 contains significant new tools to accomplish this. If they prove to be effective we shall be able to reduce the relocation load, preserve an increasing number of existing neighborhoods, and launch an effective attack upon the vast gray areas of our cities.

Rehabilitation which is cost-conscious is difficult to achieve. Even the new instruments in the 1965 legislation do not assure success. The principal problem is economic.

A given structure which may be appraised at $6,000 and requires $3,000 for rehabilitation is seldom worth $9,000 upon completion. To its owner, such an additional investment may be justified, but the security for a loan may be impaired by the lack of the property's liquidity or a low potential sales price. When and if the whole neighborhood is upgraded through widespread rehabilitation of properties, accompanied by the installation of additional and adequate community facilities and the upgrading of public services, the value of all properties will rise. This, however, takes time, and its prospect, though helpful, does not contribute enough to assure a sound economic basis for additional investments in individual structures.

An even more perplexing problem occurs in the instance of rental properties in blighted and slum areas. Some are operated by sophisticated investors who milk them, and who are not enthusiastic about lessening their returns by putting more into properties which, because of the neighborhood surroundings, cannot sustain rental increases commensurate with the increase in investment. Also, of course, where there is an upgrading of a total neighborhood, it is possible, even probable, that by charging the maximum rentals the owners will place the rehabilitated structures far beyond the paying ability of existing tenants.

Another group of investors in low-income rental properties carries a different set of problems. These are the inexperienced operators who often have paid too much for their properties and use high-cost, short-term financing. For them, as well as for sophisticated small investors who are willing to put money into their properties and are satisfied with a reasonable return, there is no solution short of refinancing with a single, long-term mortgage. Assistance in management and operation will be required for the less knowledgeable in the group.

Recognition of all these difficulties has led to the greater utilization of existing government programs[38] and the development of the new tools already mentioned. These new tools include (1) low-interest direct loans, primarily to low-income and moderate-income homeowners; (2) direct grants to homeowners of the same economic group; and (3) capital grants to nonprofit redevelopers of rental housing.[39]

Even with these instruments rehabilitation in the gray areas will continue to present problems and its progress will be difficult. In addition to the economic factors outlined above, rehabilitation will be complicated by the hesitancy of local renewal officials to undertake it and the tendency of the Federal Housing Administration to resist new principles of underwriting. The hesitancy of the local officials will reflect two principal situations: the opposition to redirecting a program and the greater effort required to carry out rehabilitation as contrasted to clearance. These situations are indigenous to any bureaucracy: change takes time and entails repudiation of past commitments. My experience suggests that if rehabilitation is approached as a practical rather than an ideological issue, results can be obtained. But the case-by-case approach is time-consuming and frequently frustrating.

There are, however, some encouraging results in rehabilitation. In Boston, for example, three large areas have been designated for such treatment and one is well underway. Other cities, including Philadelphia, Pittsburgh, New Haven, and Chicago, have had successful experiences.

I have serious doubts about using urban renewal for rehabilitation that results in high-rent housing accommodations. Experience has shown that in prestige areas, such as the East Side of New York, Georgetown in Washington, and Beacon Hill in Boston, the forces of

the private market do effect rehabilitation. Since, however, one of the generally-agreed-upon objectives of
urban renewal is to encourage better land use and reflect
good planning, there would be some legitimate employment of urban renewal for rehabilitation even if the
result would be economic displacement. This would be
justified where there were enclaves of blight destined for
higher-income occupancy, in otherwise economically
healthy areas of the city. The role of urban renewal
assistance in these instances would be to accelerate the
process of rehabilitation. Great care should be taken,
however, not to use federal funds to eliminate economic
diversity unless it is clear that market forces would result
in a spread of blight and a decline in the neighborhood.

In much current discussion of rehabilitation versus the
bulldozer there is great confusion relative to their impact
upon the present occupants of blighted areas. Either
approach, if the rehabilitated or new accommodations
are priced beyond the pocketbooks of low-income and
moderate-income families, causes displacement of the
poor and minority groups. But in urban renewal projects
those displaced are actually better off economically than
families displaced by rehabilitation undertaken outside
urban renewal areas. This follows because of the guaranteed relocation assistance. Well-motivated persons have
objected to using subsidies to displace the poor and
rehouse the affluent. What is lost sight of is that rehabilitation undertaken by private enterprise without public
assistance (as well as new construction in blighted areas
so financed) usually occasions the same type of displace-

ment, without the mitigating effect of relocation benefits.

As rehabilitation is stressed in urban renewal, demolition will decline. It will, of course, occur within rehabilitation areas where structures, either because of their condition or because of the need for open spaces or public facilities, do not lend themselves to upgrading. Also, there are some whole neighborhoods which can only be upgraded through demolition. Fewer and fewer of them will be redeveloped for upper-income occupancy in the years immediately ahead. Code enforcement will result in some demolition; some of the redeveloped areas will be utilized for new low-rent construction; and others will be used for new moderate-income accommodations.

These new directions in urban renewal will have significant consequences. In the first place, they will minimize the disruptive impact of the program; consequently, the political opposition will be reduced. More significantly, this approach will yield greater results. For, with less potential for dislocation, it will be possible to deal with large segments of the gray areas, thereby providing a basis for more effective redevelopment and more of the economically sound rehabilitation.

Thus, the new directions of the program are realistic. They will not, in and of themselves, upgrade the housing conditions of all the poor. And, indeed, urban renewal was never structured to do that, despite the legislative intent at the time of its origin. Renewal will, however, improve the quality of shelter and urban living for an increasing number of the less affluent; and, when combined with the antipoverty program, provide meaningful assistance to many of the poor.

No one federal program can, by itself, solve the social problems of the nation. Urban renewal, in the past, has too frequently complicated rather than eased these problems; in the process, however, it revealed many social issues which had been ignored. Now it is attempting to make a continuing contribution to the economic health of the central city, make the city more attractive and livable, provide sites for the housing of a diversified economic segment of the population, and upgrade the shelter and physical environment of the poor and the discriminated against.[40]

In retrospect, it seems obvious that urban renewal could never have been simultaneously the economic savior of the central city, an instrument for clearing all the slums, the means of attracting hordes of upper-middle-income families back into the central cities, and a tool for rehousing former slum dwellers in decent, safe, and sanitary housing, while generating a volume of construction involving private investments four to six times as great as the public expenditure. It could, and did, in its various aspects, do some of all of this. But the expectation that the total package would be realized through urban renewal was unrealistic from the start.

As I see it there are two dangers in the future.

The first is the existing tendency of some to cite the program's defects—real and imaginary—as a basis for doing away with it entirely. Unless there is a substitute to perform the functions that have been outlined above as the new directions of the program (and the opponents of urban renewal have no workable substitutes), we shall not save or revitalize our cities without urban renewal.

(Nor, of course, will urban renewal alone perform that feat.)

The second danger, and in many ways a more serious one, is that we will attempt to freeze the form of what is still a young and evolving program. Those who feel that urban renewal should be primarily oriented to housing (and I am in agreement with them in this belief) often conclude that downtown renewal should be stopped. But the downtown section must be vital, exciting, and economically sound for the sake of the whole city. To date downtown urban redevelopment has been a major factor in sparking the renaissance of more than a score of American cities.[41] Even Raymond Vernon, a sophisticated student of urban problems who is dubious about the future of the central city, recognizes the potential for downtown redevelopment.[42]

Over a period of fifteen years urban renewal has changed a great deal. It is important that it remain flexible, and it is vital that we question constantly its assumptions and performances. It is not the magic some who are devoted to it would have us believe. It does not solve all the problems of the central cities in and of itself. Indeed, alone, it does not solve any one of these problems. But it does perform certain functions that are indispensable and it is beginning to perform others. Let us give more attention to defining its fundamental objectives. Let us realistically integrate it into the myriad of programs which affect the urban environment. And then let us evaluate, modify, and improve urban renewal.

Its task is to assist in preserving our cities. And they are worth preserving. Charles Abrams has eloquently expressed the issue: "Despite its losses of population and its setbacks, the city remains the concourse of the various— in faces, in trade, in the exchange of thought, and in the potentials for leadership. It continues to serve its role as a refuge for the underprivileged and for those seeking richer opportunities. It is still the citadel of American freedom, in which there is greater opportunity and where the greater variety of jobs enables one to select a skill and realize an aspiration." [43]

4

DILEMMAS OF RACE

IT IS GENERALLY recognized that race is a principal factor in many aspects of urban development. James Q. Wilson, for example, identifies the color issue as one of the three major problems of our cities,[1] and Charles E. Silberman has observed that "the urban problem is in large measure a Negro problem."[2]

Government at all levels is addressing itself more and more to racial policy in housing; and civil rights groups, as well as citizens' committees, are busily engaged in pressing for equal opportunity in housing. Nonwhites and those concerned with eradicating poverty are championing more and better housing for the disadvantaged at the same time that many of them are highly critical of racial ghetto patterns of living.

Some, whose main concern is other than housing or poverty, become involved because of the pervasive impact of racial residential patterns. Proponents of school integration, for example, realize that their objective is frustrated by residential segregation; thus they become champions of integrated housing. At the same time some of the trade groups in the housing industry are equally active in attempting to prevent or vitiate public action for open occupancy in housing.

There are few among those seriously concerned with equal opportunity who would not insist that all ethnic groups in American society should have free access to housing throughout the communities in which they live. Ability to pay should be the only criterion for entrance, and individual acceptance of established behavior patterns should be the only requirement for continued occupancy.

If there were an adequate amount of decent shelter at prices which those in the market can pay, obviously a much larger proportion of the population could find "standard" accommodations—that is, sound physical structures having adequate plumbing and sanitary facilities and sufficient space for the household affected. But we have long recognized that private enterprise, unassisted, has not, cannot, and will not provide standard housing for a large proportion of the less affluent. Thus governmental programs have been established to provide the needed assistance.

Questions arise as to what public policy should be and how effective it will be in achieving the desired results. Even more fundamental is the issue of what specifically we want to achieve. Most who speak and act from the liberal point of view would probably assert that they want more and better housing available to nonwhites, a dissolvement of ghettos, and integrated residential patterns. But few have taken the time to inquire whether or not these necessarily are consistent goals. If some of these objectives are now competitive with others, or if inflexible commitment to one may delay another, which is to be selected? On what basis is it to be chosen, and by whom? Or, finally, is this a matter of one approach versus another, or the most desirable mixture of approaches?

As long as there was little effective action in this sphere of American life, such questions were academic. Today when there is action and when changes are occurring, the answers become extremely important. If, for example, rapid development of stable integrated neighborhoods will do only little to increase the supply of decent houses for nonwhites in the foreseeable future, is such action more important and socially desirable than rapid expansion of housing opportunities for nonwhites at the cost of meaningful (as contrasted to transitional) integration? On the other hand, in light of the influence of upper-class suburbia upon our values, can suburban patterns of racial occupancy be neglected?

A part of the problem is a difference of opinion as to how governmental housing programs operate and their impact upon racial residential patterns. Urban renewal offers a good example, for, as Lyle E. Schaller, a perceptive observer of the program, observed: "Thousands of Negroes think of . . . [it] as a synonym for 'Negro removal' while many whites are thoroughly convinced that their block would have remained all white if it had not been for urban renewal. Integrationists contend that urban renewal officials have been negligent by not pushing fair housing policies while segregationists read the open occupancy clauses written into redevelopment contracts and are convinced that urban renewal is but another device developed by the federal bureaucracy to break down the separation of the races." [3]

Public housing is criticized because it does not yet have a firm policy of making certain that locations are chosen to encourage integration.[4] And Whitney Young, Executive Director of the National Urban League, has stated that urban renewal, slum clearance, and highway construction will result in Negroes' being more segregated in the unattractive areas of the city.[5]

Actually, during the decade 1950 to 1960, the degree of racial residential segregation did not increase; it declined slightly. In addition, its incidence grew in the cities of the South and lessened slightly in the North,[6] reflecting the greater political power of nonwhites in the North and the utilization of residential segregation in the South as a means of vitiating judicial action that prohibits segregation in public facilities, especially public schools. During the ten years from 1950 to 1960, over-all progress toward open occupancy was slight, and my observations would lead me to believe that although it has been accelerated since 1960, the amount of interracial housing has remained quantitatively small. Yet there are unmistakable evidences of changing patterns and changing attitudes toward nonwhite neighbors.[7] The situation is not static and, as in many aspects of race relations, statistical averages and index numbers do not reflect the total situation.

Not only has there been a liberalization of attitude toward open occupancy but significant institutional developments have occurred. The first of these is the recent spontaneous rise of about a thousand fair housing committees, largely in the suburbs. These are groups of middle-class whites who have organized to recruit and welcome nonwhites as neighbors. President Kennedy's Executive Order on Equal Opportunity in Housing (1962), despite its limited coverage, has slowly opened new neighborhoods to nonwhites, supplementing the eighteen state laws, three territory laws, and thirty-four municipal ordinances for fair housing practices. Most recently, several thousand Americans have organized to provide financial resources in support of nonsegregated housing on a national scale.[8] It is important to observe that, for reasons that will be discussed later, most of the progress toward open occupancy in housing has involved the more affluent.*

---

* Unfortunately there are no comprehensive data reflecting the efficacy of fair housing committees, state and local open occupancy laws, and the Executive Order on Equal Opportunity in Housing. There are, however, fragmentary reports which demonstrate that changes are occurring, albeit slowly. During the two years ending January 1965, slightly over 100 Negro families had moved into previously all-white neighborhoods in suburbs of Maryland and Virginia which surround Washington, D.C. By June 1965 the number was just short of 200. According to the American Friends Service Committee, which has spearheaded the program, homes purchased by Negroes in these neighborhoods ranged in cost from $11,200 to $40,000 and higher. The average price was in the low $20,000 range.

In the New York metropolitan area, the movement of nonwhites into new suburban areas has been accelerated during the same period. In Chicago, too, a similar development is reported. And in these three localities, as well as scores of others, nonwhites were moving into new neighborhoods in the central city. Local groups, such as Neighbors Incorporated in Washington, were often waging campaigns to discourage the departure of whites and encourage the entrance of whites

Of all the industry groups in housing, the National Association of Real Estate Boards has been the most outspoken foe of fair housing legislation. It justifies its position on the ground of concern for property rights and freedom of choice in the disposition of real estate. State and local real estate boards have supplemented the widespread activities of the national body in this field. For example, the California organization of real estate boards drew up the language and supplied the principal support for Proposition 14 in that state, a proposition which not only prevents enforcement of the state fair housing law but also requires a statewide referendum before any additional legislation in this field can be enacted.*

Early in March 1965 the lobbyist for the Texas Real Estate Association identified himself and his organization as the proponents of a similar constitutional amendment in Texas. Texas has no fair housing legislation; so in this case the proposed amendment was designed to prevent passage of such a law.[9] This legislation was killed in committee. Nine additional states had similar legislation before them in the spring of 1965, and in every instance it had

---

into racially mixed areas. For the most part their successes seem destined to be short-lived unless the suburbs absorb nonwhites much more rapidly than they are now doing.

Each month FHA reports the opening of approximately a score of new suburban developments to nonwhites and the purchase of a hundred or so houses by nonwhites in previously all-white neighborhoods. The latter are from the inventory of properties repossessed by FHA and the Veterans Administration.

* The constitutionality of the proposition was promptly challenged. At the time of this writing the issue was before the Supreme Court of California.

strong support from the state real estate boards. However, by June none of these bills had been passed.

Local real estate boards have supported similar action in Akron, Dayton, and elsewhere. Yet there have been a few exceptions among real estate boards. Several years ago the Real Estate Board of Greater Boston was a champion of fair housing legislation in Massachusetts, and, more recently, the Real Estate Board of Greater Baltimore urged extension of the Executive Order for Equal Opportunity in Housing to include conventional lending on home mortgages by federally chartered and insured institutions.

Concurrently the masses of nonwhites, keenly conscious of their housing deprivations, press to remove them. Thus there is, within the Negro community, growing pressure for relief, and the riots in Negro ghettos during the summer of 1964 were unmistakable expressions that tempers had grown short.

All of the efforts which improve the status of low-income Americans will also affect racial housing problems. As the antipoverty program succeeds, an increasing number of nonwhites not only will have more money to spend for housing but will develop even greater dissatisfaction with their present shelter and neighborhoods.

In such a setting, it is not enough to report that attitudes and patterns are changing. For men and women who are living under intolerable conditions, such changes seem remote. They want action, and for them action is significant only if it upgrades their own housing.

Relaxation of racial ghetto patterns of living will have

immediate impact primarily upon those nonwhites who are more affluent. Such a development might have offered hope for all nonwhites had it happened a generation ago. Today the tempo in civil rights is such that these relaxations in the color line, as important as they may be over the long run, do little to reduce the social pressure in the ghettos.

There is a new realization in many parts of American society that existing racial housing patterns throughout the urban complex are crucial. Bernard Weissbourd, president of Chicago's Metropolitan Structures and a large-scale builder and redeveloper, writing for the Center for the Study of Democratic Institutions, aptly stated:

"Present segregation practices are a serious obstacle ... ; at the same time they provide an additional reason why a program designed to create heterogeneous communities both within the city and beyond the suburbs has become imperative . . . The question of segregation is always present when the character and location of public housing and urban renewal projects are being determined. An unwillingness to face up to it has paralyzed city planning. It is necessary to deal with the question not only for the sake of civil rights for Negroes but in order to free city planning from some unspoken assumptions that underlie almost everything that happens about housing in our cities." [10]

CURRENT PARADOXES

Urban renewal is the one public activity occasioning large-scale dislocation that has high standards for relocation. And it is now enforcing them.[11] Yet is the *one* public program which is constantly criticized for its relocation activities, largely in terms of their impact upon minorities.

Proponents of racial integration in housing oppose slum clearance and, frequently, advocate rehabilitation of existing structures; but rehabilitation tends to perpetuate existing residential racial patterns. Some of those who attack ghetto patterns demand that housing built in redevelopment areas be exclusively for low-income occupancy; still, in cities with large nonwhite populations, such housing usually becomes predominantly, or exclusively, nonwhite.

In an effort to break down racial concentrations, some groups look to dispersion of displacees into integrated neighborhoods. Unfortunately, the consequence of their efforts, if successful, is, sometimes, to expand the patterns of residential segregation over a larger segment of the city.

In one community or in one area, urban renewal is opposed because it is said to mean nonwhite displacement; in another its defeat is lamented because lack of urban renewal is said to be sure to cause nonwhite displacement.

Some who champion open occupancy would utilize "benign" quotas to achieve racial integration; others eschew the use of quotas, citing the ideological conflict between quotas and the concept of open occupancy.

In many cities, fair housing committees bemoan the paucity of takers among nonwhites. Yet these committees concentrate for the most part upon the placement of upper-income nonwhites. Regardless of the reasons for this (and there may be a rational basis for it, given the committees' objectives), by neglecting lower-income minority families the committees automatically limit their potential.[12]

The most stable interracial neighborhoods are inhabited by upper-income nonwhites. Such areas, while promoting racial integration, do little directly to upgrade the housing of the mass of nonwhites.

We should not be surprised by these paradoxes of race in the field of housing or in other aspects of our society. *There are problems of race because there is prejudice. And prejudice is always irrational and illogical. Those who are the butt of extreme prejudice can hardly be expected to react in terms of detached logic. Nor do consistent lines of approach emerge from these circumstances.*

THE PROBLEMS OF SITES

The paradoxes just listed now must be examined in more detail.

The *location* of housing is perhaps the most crucial single factor in its racial occupancy. If new residential construction or rehabilitation is carried out in a site which is an integral part of nonwhite concentration, the occupancy usually becomes either exclusively or almost exclusively nonwhite. The one general exception occurs where an entire neighborhood is cleared and a new (and higher) income group is housed there.

These circumstances have led to the current pressure from civil rights and associated groups to secure locations for public housing beyond the boundaries of existing nonwhite neighborhoods. Several problems emerge.

The first problem is a reflection of both class and racial attitudes. Regardless of color, the residents of middle-income neighborhoods generally oppose the location of public housing projects in their midst. In addition, white neighborhoods of all income composition usually oppose such projects on the basis of racial concerns. Emulating largely the attitudes of upper-income groups and reflecting the racial exclusiveness of suburbia, most residents of white areas oppose public housing primarily because they fear nonwhite inundation.[13] And all of this is complicated by the fact that because of the very racial attitudes that have led to residential segregation, public housing projects having a policy of open occupancy frequently become predominantly, or exclusively, nonwhite.[14] In small communities with limited nonwhite populations, or in developments removed from concentrations of nonwhites, this need not occur. Where it does happen, however, it, in turn, accentuates the fears delineated above.

Selection of sites for public housing is primarily a local responsibility, but the Public Housing Administration now lists promotion of racially democratic housing patterns as one criterion. This is sometimes effective; it does not, however, guarantee locations which will facilitate mixed racial patterns. Though the federal government can refuse to approve a site, it cannot take the initiative and select one.

Situations increasingly arise where a locality will approve for public housing only sites now occupied by nonwhites or in areas undergoing racial transition. The choice for local groups concerned with housing for low-income and nonwhite families is often between (1) public housing that will be primarily nonwhite and (2) only a small amount of new low-income public housing. The principal impact of federal policy in this situation comes out of its requirement that those displaced by urban renewal and public housing be relocated in decent, safe, and sanitary accommodations. Often this requirement cannot be met without additional public housing. Usually it is facilitated if such low-rent housing is constructed on vacant land, most of which is outside existing nonwhite neighborhoods.

The selection of vacant sites is, of course, desirable from many points of view. It avoids dislocation; it provides a net expansion in the supply of low-rent accommodations; it relieves the pressures of a growing nonwhite population upon the existing supply of housing as was noted above. But, since public housing is initiated by local governments, there are slight prospects of its being constructed in the suburbs. Within the central city, the supply of vacant land is often restricted, and most that exists is so located as to assure strong opposition to public housing. Yet sound housing policy would dictate use of vacant sites or those that are appropriate for residential redevelopment but now in other uses.

The greatest progress toward integration in public housing is occurring in existing projects which were formerly tenanted exclusively by one racial group. As a consequence of the Executive Order on Equal Opportunity in Housing, a few changes were made. Under Section VI of the Civil Rights Act of 1964, all local housing authorities must agree to open occupancy in all public housing accommodations. Already the pace of integration has been stepped up. Interestingly, had there been an open-occupancy policy at the time the affected projects were constructed, many of the developments now subject to integration would never have been built.

The resolving of issues about sites for public housing brings to the surface differences in outlook between the more affluent nonwhites and the less affluent ones. The affluent tend to be more insistent on integration, whereas the less affluent may feel that their primary need is more decent housing and their situation so critical that they cannot afford the luxury of pressing for integration. When public housing outside, but not far removed from, nonwhite concentration becomes increasingly occupied by nonwhites, as it frequently does, little is gained for integration, but the supply of shelter and the land area available to low-income nonwhites is augmented. As a practical matter, in some localities there are relatively few sites available to public housing today which will assure stable interracial occupancy. Thus the dilemma.

I have noted above that when the advent of nonwhite residents accelerates abandonment of an area by whites, the cause of residential integration is set back. To meet this issue voluntary groups are sometimes formed to discourage panic selling and abandonment of established neighborhoods by white residents; and such action presents no dilemmas. But there are a few people who would restrain rather than merely discourage the movement of whites. This, of course, is inconsistent with our announced concern for maximum freedom of choice in selecting a place to live. And, unfortunately, it would frequently serve to delay the expansion of housing available to nonwhites. For under current patterns of racially homogeneous neighborhoods, the principal method used by nonwhites to augment the supply of shelter available to them is to succeed or displace whites. The only effective way to discourage panic selling and rapid racial succession in neighborhoods is to secure *de facto* open occupancy in a wide sector of the housing market. When that is achieved, all will be able to move freely but the exercise of this choice will not assure residence in a permanently ethnically homogeneous neighborhood: thus the racial motivation for moving will be greatly reduced.

There is real irony in that urban renewal, a program identified on the basis of its earlier performance as "Negro clearance," has recently made some significant contributions toward desirable sites for public housing. Many of these have been so redeveloped as to encourage biracial occupancy. To date, the volume of public housing on urban renewal sites has not been quantitatively or relatively large. It is, however, growing. Prior to the fiscal year ending June 30, 1961, contracts for public housing in urban renewal areas had been signed for 66 projects involving 12,098 dwelling units. During the succeeding three years between 1961 and 1964, 117 additional ones involving 14,988 dwelling units were placed under contract. More important, the patterns of occupancy which evolve are significant. Biracial occupancy of public housing occurred in the urban renewal programs of a score of cities, including Louisville and Newport, in Kentucky; Easton, Farrell, and Philadelphia, in Pennsylvania; New York City; Minneapolis; and Morristown, New Jersey.

Urban renewal has made its greatest contribution to the site problem in the realm of moderate-income housing. Here the relative demand among nonwhites for housing is not so overwhelming as to offer the same threat of inundation by the minorities. In addition, there is a sizable white demand at this income level. Thus, the moderate-income housing program referred to in Chapter 3, which provides housing bargains through below-the-market interest rates on long-term mortgages, is economically attractive to whites as well as nonwhites. Since the program began in 1961 an increasing volume of this housing has been planned, built, and occupied in urban renewal areas. A significant segment of it is racially mixed and appears to be fairly stable in this respect.[15]

The reason why the most stable biracial neighborhoods are those of upper-income occupancy is that the possibility of nonwhite inundation is less real, reflecting the relative paucity of higher-income nonwhites in most cities. Unquestionably stable interracial neighborhoods have emerged in Washington, St. Louis, New York City, Boston, Chicago, Detroit, New Haven, Jersey City, Newark, Paterson, Philadelphia, Harrisburg, York, Minneapolis, San Francisco, Richmond (California), and in a growing number of redevelopments elsewhere.

Even in the South, urban renewal has facilitated new racial patterns. In the Landmark luxury apartments constructed in the Butler Street urban renewal site in Atlanta, Georgia, two Negro families were in occupancy in February 1965. In the redevelopment of East Nashville, three Negro households were living in a new downtown apartment building. In these and other cities of the South the novelty is not interracial patterns of living, but such patterns in newly constructed high-income and moderate-income neighborhoods.

As of June 30, 1964, some 54,875 dwelling units in urban renewal areas were occupied. About 90 percent had been privately financed; the rest were public housing. Whites lived in 32,796 units, nonwhites in 19,617, and color was not reported in the remaining 2,462. Thirty-five projects had all-white occupancy, thirty-six were occupied exclusively by nonwhites, and ninety-three had some degree of racial mixture. Fourteen of these "mixed" developments with 7,077 dwelling units were from 95 to 99 percent white; seven were 95 to 99 percent nonwhite; and seventy-two, housing 35,528 households, were integrated in the sense that over 5 percent of the occupants were of a second ethnic origin. These "integrated" developments housed some 22,000 white and 11,000 nonwhite families. The developments for which race was not reported were located in Puerto Rico; they housed some 2,500 additional families and were racially integrated. These data are the basis of my earlier observation that "urban renewal is providing, for the first time, a sizable supply of new racially integrated housing in a growing number of our cities . . . [It] is slowly affording non-whites (most of whom are middle-income) a chance to move out of racial ghettos into what, for the most part, seem to be stable ethnically integrated neighborhoods. Non-white families involved—far too few to date—are thereby able at long last to begin to emulate the residential mobility of earlier migrants to urban centers.[16]

Although this may offer some encouragement to integrationists, it has extracted a real cost, the impact of which has been concentrated upon low-income non-whites. The first element, of course, is the forced displacement of households and small businesses. In addition, urban renewal has torn down ten times more low-income and moderate-income housing units than it has helped to produce. Until recently, most redevelopment housing has been so highly priced as either to exclude or greatly restrict nonwhite occupancy.[17]

An interesting dilemma faces efforts to effect open occupancy in new construction facilitated by the Veterans Administration and the Federal Housing Administration. It has been suggested that such construction should be identified by a sign which would announce its availability to all ethnic groups. Aside from the technical difficulty inherent in the fact that a given development may use several types of financing (including conventional, which is not now covered by the Executive Order), there are policy questions. With less than 20 percent of new starts now affected by federal open-occupancy requirements, such signs might discourage white purchasers or renters (who would go to competing developments). Were the coverage of the Executive Order more extensive, this problem would be less troublesome. But, if the coverage were more extensive, signs of identification might not be necessary, since nonwhite purchasers or renters could assume that any new project would be available to them and behave accordingly.

In any discussion of site selection, a word should be added about the relative desirability of existing ghettos for redevelopment. Because of the historic concentration of newcomers near the core of the city and the long-time occupancy of desirably located sites by nonwhites, particularly in cities of the Old South, theirs are often prime locations. Proposals to clear such sites (and low-income racially mixed sites) and rehouse higher-income whites on them were the basis for coining the phrases "Negro removal" and "Negro clearance." Yet at the very moment that nonwhites and others opposed such action, some of them also opposed the redevelopment (either with or without urban renewal) of these areas with public housing.

INCOME AND INTEGRATION

The basic urban dilemma of income and race has already been mentioned. It is a choice between (1) housing a large number of nonwhites in low-rent accommodations, (2) housing a somewhat smaller number in moderate-income housing, and (3) housing a much smaller number in high-income structures. This dilemma is most sharply presented when decisions are being made relative to the income distribution to be achieved in the redevelopment of an urban renewal area, although it exists also when construction occurs elsewhere. There is, of course, an option of some of each type of housing, but it is seldom considered by those who engage in this colloquy. Because the degree and the potential stability of racial mixture varies, in any one site, inversely with the level of income served by redevelopment, the choice, again, frequently appears to be between racial integration and the augmentation of new housing available to non-whites. This issue presents itself in several forms.

In a Midwestern city where a vast urban renewal project is largely completed, and where half of the newly constructed 3,700 dwelling units are occupied by non-whites, there was a question about income groups to be served by the future construction on the remaining un-developed land. Originally it was proposed that over half the additional new units should be for moderate-income households. The redevelopers of somewhat higher-rent housing now in occupancy wanted a lower proportion of moderate-income housing and a larger proportion of higher-income accommodations. The Negro com-munity was split, with most preferring the maximum degree of moderate-income housing. Civil rights groups and liberals were more sharply split.

There was no question that in proportion as a larger amount of moderate-income housing was provided, the degree of nonwhite occupancy would increase. Some feared that it might become so pronounced as to endanger the stability of the existing interracial pattern. At the same time, many who live in the vicinity of the renewal area still believe that since it was originally a Negro slum, the proportion of nonwhites rehoused should be significantly larger than it has been to date.

After much discussion and the consideration of a number of proposals, the city council finally approved the sale of thirty acres in the urban renewal areas. The redeveloper will construct over 1,100 dwelling units in high-rise apartments and town houses. Up until the final action of the city council, the economic mix of the redevelopment remained fluid. At the end there was a relaxation from the previous requirement of 55 percent moderate-income accommodations; the contract with the developer specified no more than 40 percent and no less than 20 percent of such housing.

This apparent imbalance was partially offset by the plans for moderate-income construction elsewhere in the area of nonwhite concentration. By June 1965 some 1,200 units of 221(d)(3) housing was completed, under construction, or planned for this section of the city.

In a somewhat smaller city in the East a different manifestation of the same problem has arisen. As in the Midwestern community, the renewal area was previously a Negro slum. Original plans envisioned redevelopment for high-income occupancy. This occasioned a storm of protest on the part of civil rights groups. Further analysis indicated that there would not be a market for high-income housing and plans were revised.

At this point there was a split between the protesting groups. One wanted moderate-income redevelopment on the grounds that it would provide housing within the reach of many nonwhites while lending itself to integration. Another group championed public housing because it would not occasion economic dislocation in the area.

It was decided to achieve economically diversified housing, with concentration upon moderate-income accommodations. But the controversy continued to rage. The organization and the individuals who supported the decision took the position that it would not only provide a significant volume of housing for nonwhites but also create a stable interracial neighborhood. They said that if nothing but public housing was built, the result would be an economic and ethnic ghetto. Also, they feared that it would be difficult to market integrated housing on the site of a former Negro slum if a large volume of low-income housing were provided there.

The champions of public housing redevelopment claimed that it was only equitable that the same people who previously lived in the area should move back into it. When they were told that, on the basis of past experience, only a few of the displaced would seek shelter there, they replied that the adverse impact of urban renewal had been concentrated upon poor Negroes and that this same group, suffering from a lack of decent housing, should benefit directly from the redevelopment. They added that relocation would only aggravate the shelter deprivation of this class, immediately reducing the supply of low-income housing in the city.

There were some interesting fringe benefits incident to the controversy. Relocation will take place in stages.

Redevelopment on the site will include an economically diversified range of housing, some within the means of displaced families. Relocation planning now calls for short-term property improvements within the project area to serve better the needs of those who reside there during most of the relocation period. During this interim a community center will be provided for their use, and it will offer extensive social services, including a number of programs typical of the antipoverty campaign.

One could describe many other cases in which there appears to be a choice between augmenting to the maximum degree the supply of housing for nonwhites and obtaining less housing for them while fostering integration. In some instances, as in the extensive West Side rehabilitation and redevelopment in New York, an effort is made to achieve something of both goals. Redevelopment there will provide a relatively small volume of newly constructed high-rent units, a sizable volume of new and rehabilitated middle-income and moderate-income housing, and a slightly smaller amount of low-income housing. Even this solution fails to avoid dilemmas. What, for example, should be the mix? What criteria should be selected as the basis for the decision? And these questions, if they could be answered definitely, would not be determining. Any range of choices is limited by the response of the marketplace; and a mix that might work in the West Side of Manhattan would probably not be economically possible in Harlem or the Bronx, let alone the South Side of Chicago. Experience in New York City, San Francisco, and other cities has demon-

strated that political pressure, too, exerts a significant
influence upon the ultimate decisions.

Related decisions must be faced outside urban renewal
areas. For some time public housing has been under attack. Much of the criticism is somewhat similar to the
disenchantment with urban renewal: the program failed
to realize the high hopes and promises of its earlier
proponents. This has generated great disillusionment,
and disillusionment usually leads to condemnation. The
truth is that, with all its limitations, public housing has
significantly upgraded the shelter of almost 600,000
American families, half of which are nonwhite. It has also
perpetuated economic ghettos and developed a poor
image in some localities.

In an effort to offset both of these weaknesses, many
propose mixing public and moderate-income housing.
This has a surface appeal, seeming to provide the best of
both worlds, that is, an increase in low-income housing
and at the same time the provision of racially integrated
neighborhoods. Indeed, there is a slowly growing number
of successful combinations of this type and they may
provide an arrangement which will be a viable answer in
many areas of the central cities. This is always a real
possibility in sites which are well located, such as the
West Side of Manhattan or the Western Addition area
in San Francisco.

Yet there are dilemmas here too. They cannot be
wished away, and they may as well be understood. In
those localities where there is the fear and possibility of
nonwhite inundation, the public housing sector in such

a development could easily become all nonwhite, creating a pattern that might spread to the moderate-income accommodations as well. In many areas and in many sites, serious difficulties arise in marketing an interracial moderate-income development. If such a development is confused or identified with public housing, these difficulties can be aggravated.

Thus, in an effort to achieve two laudable objectives, low-income and moderate-income housing on the one hand and integration on the other, there is the danger that neither will be accomplished. Outside urban renewal areas as well as in them, zoning relaxations and public acquisition of land for housing occur only after local public hearings. One of the questions asked at these hearings is the type of construction or redevelopment that is envisioned. In many cities, neither zoning adjustments nor utilization of eminent domain will be approved if the re-use is to include public housing. Thus its proposed mixture with moderate-income housing may defeat attempts to construct either.

As suggested above, if moderate-income housing is decided upon, it may be successful at the cost of failure to alleviate to the maximum degree the quantitative needs of nonwhites. Such construction, however, is not without a significant indirect contribution to this objective. It greatly facilitates the filter-down process. For unlike high-cost additions to the housing supply, moderate-income additions are priced fairly close to what the poor are paying for substandard housing. Thus, as the volume of such new housing increases and vacancies occur, it is possible that lower-income families may move in before the house has depreciated over a long period of time. Such depreciation, of course, is what has defeated filtering-down in the past. By the time high-priced housing has depreciated enough to be within the financial reach of the poor, it is pretty bad housing, either in terms of its physical condition or its overcrowded pattern of occupancy.

The principal existing and proposed moderate-income housing programs of the federal government are restricted to nonprofit and limited-profit sponsors for rental units, and to individual or cooperative ownership for others. Insofar as such housing is constructed in former slum areas, it will have a revolutionary impact upon the neighborhoods. A radical change in ownership results. More important, slum landlords are replaced by nonprofit or limited-profit organizations.

In certain cities, "Negro housing" is a most profitable investment: some individuals and firms operate as many as 500 units each. This large-scale ownership contrasts with the ineffectual bargaining power of poor Negro tenants and perpetuates possibilities of economic exploitation. Federally assisted moderate-income housing is a real threat to the slumlords, and they recognize it. In one state they are said to have exchanged information from city to city and to have been discussing strategy to kill any and all forms of urban renewal. In this instance slum clearance, via urban renewal, can be a real benefit to nonwhites and contribute significantly to the upgrading of housing in the affected cities. Of course, public housing has long operated to serve the same purpose.

There is a much more basic philosophical argument in favor of moderate-income housing. It starts from the premise that cities need to manufacture a middle class.[18] Moderate-income housing is consistent with the true aims of the city, according to this concept. Actually, those, like Charles Silberman, who accept this point of view would look beyond housing. "It's doubtful," he writes, "whether any simple, dramatic approach can solve the Negro housing problem. So long as the great majority of Negroes have slum incomes, they are going to live in slums. In the long run, therefore, the only way to solve the problem of Negro housing is to solve the problem of Negro people—to raise the economic and social level of the Negro community." [19]

Of course, something has to be done over the short run. An approach which would be consistent with this analysis has already been proposed. It is to utilize, through rent supplements, existing housing as a source of shelter for low-income families. This proposal, however, leans upon several assumptions. The first is that there is a supply of available housing that can be upgraded. One of two conditions would have to exist: either there would be a loose housing market or a low-income and moderate-income housing program which would encourage an easement in the housing market for less affluent families.

Recognizing the difficulties of obtaining sites for public housing, there are those who advocate a bold program for moderate-income housing. Both in the central city and, to a lesser degree in the suburbs, the problem of obtaining sites for moderate-income housing is more manageable. Thus the proponents of this approach state that if such housing is augmented, it will be possible to relieve the pressure for accommodations in the ghettos, reduce the degree of economic exploitation therein, and upgrade the supply of existing low-income housing while increasing the supply of moderate-income structures available to minorities and others.

Once this prospect is suggested, there are pressures to abolish the federal public housing program and leave low-cost construction to private nonprofit organizations. I am opposed to these pressures. In the first place, the financial formula of public housing provides a unique machinery for low-cost construction loans. This is achieved through the use of federally guaranteed tax-exempt bonds issued by local governments. With the money raised by these low-interest loans, they pay for the land and the construction of public housing developments. Secondly, the number, expertise, and capacity of nonprofit organizations in this country are still small. To look to them for exclusive or primary sponsorship, construction, and operation would automatically limit the volume of low-income housing. Finally, we are recognizing that there is a need for greater social services and humanly oriented management in low-income housing developments. Public bodies can often best provide these, and they are apt to be more readily available to public housing than to developments by nonprofit organizations.

The proposal for a bold program of moderate-income housing and an end to the public housing program is, in fact, an expression of an "either-or"—a categorically logical—solution to a problem for which there is no single solution. While we expand the medium-income housing approaches, we also need to improve and redirect the public housing program. Until the war on poverty is won, we shall continue to have many families and individuals whose housing needs can best be met by public housing.

REHABILITATION AND RACE

The increasing importance of rehabilitation in urban renewal was discussed in the preceding chapter. The initial reaction to this has been generally favorable on the part of those who decry "Negro removal." There is a question as to how long it will be popular with those whose principal concern is integration.

By its very nature rehabilitation that is cost-conscious, in the sense that it avoids pricing former residents out of the area, tends to perpetuate existing patterns of living. This means that although it would minimize the displacement of nonwhites from localities where they now live, it would contribute little to their entering new areas. But it would vastly upgrade and improve their present environment. Here the dilemma seems to be avoiding "Negro clearance" at the price of making little progress toward integration. Actually, much more is involved. Real and spurious issues of political power and questions of Negro businesses must be considered as well.

There is a prevalent attitude among Negro politicians that efforts to destroy the ghetto are designed, in part at least, to dilute the political power of nonwhites. It seems to me that this is of limited validity. In city-wide or statewide elections such concentrations are meaningless, and in precinct or other smaller area-based contests, non-whites would have greater political power if so distributed as to be deciding factors in several such contests rather than being the totality in one contest. However, the fact that such opinion exists creates a vested interest in preserving existing neighborhoods. On the other hand there is great validity in opposing minority group displacement on the grounds that it uproots and often destroys nonwhite businesses. These are usually small, somewhat marginal establishments, catering to a market peculiar to their location. Relocation is always difficult for them and often impossible.

Wide-scale rehabilitation under urban renewal requires a significant degree of neighborhood citizen participation, and the population involved is, for the most part, the same before and after the activity. Thus any economic class conflict as to objectives is minimized. The present residents want to preserve the current economic composition of the affected area. If they are lower-income renters, they usually oppose radical upgrading lest it appreciably inflate rents. Most of the occupants of the deteriorating gray areas outside the central business district, once there is the prospect of area-wide upgrading, are primarily concerned with their continued occupancy with the minimum increase in housing costs.

Proponents of integration may react differently. Rehabilitation of the gray areas with a concern for avoiding displacement of former residents will, ultimately, have effects somewhat similar to building public housing in nonwhite neighborhoods: it will tend to perpetuate economic and ethnic ghettos. But it will not cause the same degree of economic and ethnic displacement that widespread rebuilding will cause, nor will it create a physical setting that will last for sixty years, as public housing construction will create. It may be, therefore, that the proponents of integration will find rehabilitation under urban renewal more palatable than demolition, relocation, and redevelopment. Indeed some socially motivated organizations are championing rehabilitation and residential integration as complementary goals.[20]

There is, of course, less chance of whites' moving into an area that was once a nonwhite slum if its former residents remain after rehabilitation than when it is demolished and both the physical and human symbols of its past are removed. Where there are pockets of low-income nonwhite concentration, rehabilitation that prices former residents out of the market can, and has, become a tool for minority displacement.

Thus rehabilitation can occasion controversy over racial patterns. For example, in the Hyde Park area of Chicago, redevelopment which involved much "spot rehabilitation" was criticized because it had failed to rehouse a large proportion of low-income nonwhite residents.[21] A crusading Negro champion of civil rights challenged this criticism, affirming that the redevelopment in Hyde Park was making a basic contribution to residential integration in Chicago. Actually, he was right; but there had been displacement of low-income nonwhites at the same time that higher-income Negroes entered the area. Here, it seems, the effect of rehabilitation was similar to that of new construction, reflecting the impact of the cost of the housing provided.

In Washington, D.C., an urban renewal plan featuring rehabilitation was supported by low-income residents. This came to public notice when the National Capital Planning Commission rejected the long-discussed Adams-Morgan urban renewal proposal calling for spot clearance and spot rehabilitation in a large area of Northwest Washington. Most of the low-income Negro residents in the proposed project area, many liberals, the local Negro press (which frequently characterized urban renewal as "Negro clearance"), as well as the leading daily paper, deplored the Planning Commission's action.[22] The small businesses in the area, a private so-called rehabilitation firm, and some resident upper-income nonwhites applauded it.[23]

These different reactions followed from the fact that the renewal plan would have provided low-income and moderate-income housing for many of the present less affluent Negro residents in the area. The forces of the private market and code enforcement, which the Planning Commission expected to carry out the upgrading of the area, would dislocate permanently many of the low-income residents without giving them any relocation assistance. These forces would also permit many small businesses to remain—business that would be displaced or forced to remodel by any effective site plan concerned with compatible land-use patterns.

If an area is in nonwhite occupancy, it cannot become

integrated without some displacement, even if the treatment is code enforcement or rehabilitation. The situation is complicated by the fact that urban renewal has been used as an instrument for displacing all—or most—nonwhites from desirable areas of a city. Although this seldom happens today, the fact that it has happened created an image of the program. Thus any displacement of nonwhites automatically conjures up the concept of pushing minorities out of desirable locations—and usually without any compensation for the inconvenience.

One may conjecture that of all the possible compromises in racial housing issues, the compromise that will be least difficult to live with, for now, will be rehabilitation. This will be true, however, only if the real impact of this approach is realized—an understanding which I doubt exists today. The point is that, provided this approach is supplemented by positive action to achieve the objectives of democratic housing patterns elsewhere in a community, rehabilitation which avoids general economic displacement is not too damaging to these goals.

MEETING THE HOUSING NEEDS OF NONWHITES

It requires no detailed analysis to demonstrate that in our urban centers where the nonwhite population is growing, now primarily because of natural increase rather than migration, adequate housing for minorities can be obtained only by expanding the space they occupy. Additional pressures are generated by new highway construction and urban renewal, as well as additional locally sponsored programs which displace nonwhites. But, so far, stable biracial residential patterns seem to require gradual change in neighborhood ethnic composition, and that, *if restricted to only a few parts of a city*, results in too slow a pace of change to provide the volume of housing needed by nonwhites.

One device suggested to ease the situation is the entrance of nonwhites into the suburbs. So far this has been a trickle, limited primarily to the more affluent. A more fundamental approach, outlined above, would be to provide a large volume of lower-cost housing on an open-occupancy basis in the suburbs. Both economic and psychological benefits would follow. The economic benefits have been shown earlier in this chapter. Equally important would be the resulting modification of the homogeneous patterns of suburbia and the tendency to reduce the prestige of such residential arrangements throughout the urban complex. There would be other benefits as well. In Chapter 2, I referred to the costs of continued exclusion of lower-income families from the suburbs. Also, as more and more employment opportunities appear outside the central cities, such exclusion accentuates the already serious problems of transportation.

But, in addition to white suburbia's opposition to non-white neighbors, there are complications to the outward-movement approach, too. An immediate one is the apparent disinclination of many nonwhites to move away from the central city. This may be a short-run phenomenon, reflecting the cultural security the ghetto affords to many who feel rejected elsewhere; it is an adjustment to enforced residential segregation. In any event, there is

nothing innate about the behavior and if new opportunities were to arise, it is probable that they would be
embraced by the majority who may be hesitant to pioneer
today.

Some upper-income nonwhites do have a strong attachment to their present central-city locations.[24] They
have economic, political, and social motivations for remaining in a nonwhite community. But a much larger
number of lower-income persons who are economically
and socially mobile probably have lesser ties with the
ghetto and provide a much greater potential for movement to the suburbs. Certainly, as a recent article reminds
us, there is a real possibility that the opening of lower-
income housing to nonwhites in the suburbs would significantly ease the quantitative pressure on housing in the
central cities while not necessarily raising issues of color
and class simultaneously in suburbia. This suggests that
the middle-class orientation of most fair housing committees has greatly limited their efficacy.[25]

It suggests, also, a redirection of the committees' programs. This would be consistent with recent advocacy
of a more effective spatial distribution of higher-income
nonwhites—one which would involve their continued
occupancy in the central city. For some time most nonwhites will be central-city residents. It is claimed, therefore, that the better-trained and more successful nonwhites can be most helpful in accelerating the movement
of other nonwhites into the mainstream of American life
by remaining in those parts of the metropolitan areas
where nonwhites are concentrated.[26]

Again the issue does not call for an "either-or" approach but one that involves both phenomena. Actually, regardless of ideology, both are occurring and increasingly will occur. In Boston, for example, the older, long-term middle-class residents of a Negro area undergoing rehabilitation and redevelopment indicated a preference to remain there. The younger, better-trained, and occupationally integrated households were the pioneers in entering suburban and central-city biracial neighborhoods.[27]

As we move toward realization of widespread open occupancy—the only residential pattern consistent with the philosophy and promise of a democracy—we shall encounter many contradictory developments. There will be frequent instances when efforts to achieve a stated objective may result in the realization of another. Or we may achieve one goal without contributing significantly to another equally important one. Perhaps the most frustrating development will be occasions when mixed racial residential patterns that have involved great dedication and effort will prove to be but transitional stages in the process of augmenting the inventory of shelter available to nonwhites.

But without abandoning or repudiating our commitment to equal opportunity in housing, we cannot ignore the supply of existing facilities. This is no less valid in housing than in education. For both, there is wisdom in Kenneth Clark's recent dictum that the goals of integration and quality of existing facilities must be sought together.[28] In both of these basic areas of American life, each supports the other.

5

SUMMING UP

I HAVE REPEATEDLY URGED a federal urban land policy. Others have noted the lack of a deliberate policy guidance in national housing programs. Thus William Nash and Chester Hartman assert: "If our central concern really is to provide decent homes and suitable living environments for all families, then a wholly different strategy and a wholly revised set of priorities are called for." [1] Concurrently, there has been a call for federal leadership and affirmative action in the field of race and housing.

We are moving slowly toward facing up to the issue of urban land policy. President Johnson's message on "The Problems and Future of the Central City and Its Suburbs" (March 2, 1965) represented a significant step forward. It emphasized metropolitan-area planning. The President also called for financial assistance for (1) area-wide water and sewerage facilities, (2) advanced acquisition of land for public uses, and (3) new communities and planned subdivisions. He proposed an Institute of Urban Development and a Temporary National Commission on Codes, Zoning, Taxation, and Development

Standards. The direction of federal land policy has been set.

The mixture of private industry and government in this field and the absence of viable local governments in areas where land policy is needed dictate a certain degree of trial and error. In many instances the approach will have to be indirect, providing rewards for desirable patterns rather than prohibiting undesirable ones. Often, there will be no local governmental bodies willing, able, and ready to regulate. And the expression of individual choices, operating as it does through the private sector, further limits the possibility of public directives. It also affects the type of housing program that can be successfully carried out, influencing significantly the degree of economic and ethnic class mixture.

It will be necessary to encourage and facilitate state as well as federal concern for urban land usage. The federal government can help by continually articulating problems through conferences, statements by the President and his official family, Congressional hearings, and legislative action. It can also provide financial assistance for the encouragement of more effective state machinery and for the partial support of state programs.

At the same time reapportionment should bring about more state action affecting urbanization. This will probably be concentrated in the suburbs and the urbanizing areas beyond. It is in just these areas that there is today a vacuum of urban-oriented government and the greatest need for rational utilization of land. One may hope that the recent emphasis of federal policy upon comprehensive and metropolitan planning may rub off on the states. Certainly the federal government can and should continue to encourage this through selective and well-directed financial assistance.

Housing policy, too, is being revised. There is greater coordination between those agencies of the federal government which provide financial support for urban renewal and mortgage underwriting for housing; and more and more attention is being paid to the sectors of the market whose members cannot secure decent shelter without some form of public assistance. We are revising our priorities in this sphere, placing new emphasis upon low-income and moderate-income housing and rehabilitation.

In Chapter 3, I set forth the recent changes of policy and emphasis in urban renewal. The new directions are part and parcel of the evolving system of new priorities in housing. They assume more definitive shape in urban renewal, both because of the degree of federal financial involvement and the existence of effective city governments. Most important, the new directions in urban renewal will bring about a greater capacity of cities to absorb more comprehensive programs. Thus, we shall be able to expand the activity at the same time that its impact spreads from slums and downtown blight to the vast gray areas.

Issuance of the Executive Order on Equal Opportunity in Housing in 1962 was the first comprehensive action to secure open occupancy in federally assisted housing. It was supplemented and supported by Title VI of the Civil

Rights Act of 1964. Because of the paradoxes and the dilemmas in race and housing, we must move simultaneously in two directions. First, as a matter of simple justice, as a means of avoiding future violence, and as an instrument for preserving our cities, the supply of decent low-income and moderate-income housing must be increased—and it must be available to minorities on an equal basis. Concurrently, patterns of racial integration in housing must be rapidly augmented; such patterns are a principal means of breaking down enforced racial segregation. Racial segregation is not only the symbol of discrimination in housing but also the institution which limits nonwhites' housing choices and exposes so many to economic exploitation, social differentiation, and exclusion from racially integrated public facilities and accommodations.

Thus, it appears that in each of the basic phases of urban development treated in this book, we are moving toward a national policy.

Because of the heterogeneity of the country, its governmental structure, our traditions relative to land and home ownership, and the paradoxes in race and housing, definitive formulations of policy are difficult. *If there is a single theme that runs through this book it is this: we must avoid doctrinaire approaches. There are no simple answers. Indeed, there are few single answers or pat solutions which will be effective.*

Unique situations confront us as we effect the transition from a rural to an urban nation. Many have been outlined in this book, and one should be mentioned again. It is that in the United States we shall attempt to meet the problems involved through a partnership between private enterprise and government. As was suggested earlier, few, if any, models in other nations can be adopted completely. At the same time, there are many approaches abroad which should and can indicate pitfalls and objectives.[2] But what we develop will be an indigenous American product, responsive to our people, institutions, and resources.

As difficult, cumbersome, and frequently obsolete as it is, we have some machinery for meeting the future problems of urban development. And we are developing additional and more effective machinery. A basic issue is our ability to recognize the nature of rapid urbanization and the necessity for sound objectives and programs to deal with it. Provided we avoid esoteric controversy about government versus private enterprise, there is every reason to believe that we can develop an urban setting which will be responsive to the needs of an urban society.

NOTES AND INDEX

NOTES AND INDEX

NOTES

CHAPTER 1: URBANIZATION

1. James Reston, "A Whirlwind of Caution in the White House," *New York Times*, Dec. 16, 1964.

CHAPTER 2: NEW COMMUNITIES

1. Oscar Handlin, "The Modern City as a Field of Historical Study," in *The Historian and the City*, ed. Oscar Handlin and John Burchard (Cambridge, Mass.: M.I.T. Press and Harvard University Press, 1963), p. 25.

2. Herbert J. Gans, "Effects of the Move from City to Suburb," in *The Urban Condition*, ed. Leonard J. Duhl (New York: Basic Books, 1963), p. 193.

3. There is much literature on the appeal of the suburbs to Americans. For an eloquent statement on this subject, see David Riesman, "The Suburban Dislocation," *Annals of the American Academy of Political and Social Science*, November 1957, pp. 123–146.

4. William H. Whyte, Jr., *Man and the Modern City* (Pittsburgh: University of Pittsburgh Press, 1963), p. 49.

5. *The English New Town* (New York: Bowery Savings Bank, 1953), pp. 5, 3, 7–8.

6. Albert Mayer, "Architecture as Total Community: The Challenge Ahead," *Architectural Record*, August 1964, pp. 129–138, and September 1964, pp. 197–206. Mr. Mayer is a long-time expositor and proponent of new towns. See the following of his articles: "A New-Town Program," *American Institute of Architects Journal*, January 1951, pp. 5–10; "Trends in New Town

Development," in *Planning 1952* (Chicago: American Society of Planning Officials, 1952), pp. 64–71.

7. Dennis O'Harrow, "New Towns or New Sprawl?" *ASPO Newsletter*, October 1964.

8. Sir Frederic Osborn and Arnold Whittick, *The New Towns: The Answer to Megalopolis* (London: McGraw-Hill, 1963).

9. Lewis Mumford, "Introduction," in Osborn and Whittick, just cited, pp. 2–3.

10. *Ibid.*, pp. 4–5.

11. Osborn and Whittick, pp. 20, 64, 69, 115.

12. *Ibid.*, pp. 23, 77.

13. *Ibid.*, pp. 32, 61, 87.

14. *Ibid.*, p. 73.

15. *Ibid.*, pp. 88–89.

16. Marion Clawson, *Man and Land in the United States* (Lincoln: University of Nebraska Press, 1964), p. 37.

17. *Ibid.*, pp. 64, 65.

18. For an account of the evolution of national land policy, see R. C. Weaver, "National Land Policies—Historic and Emergent," *UCLA Law Review*, March 1965, pp. 719–733.

19. See, for example, Angus Wilson, *Late Call* (New York: Viking Press, 1964). This British novel has as its setting an English new town. The author dissects the institution. He indicates that it is better than the environment of the heroine several generations ago in an urban slum and in a society of overt class differentiation. But he depicted the new town as no more of a Utopia than our novelists often attribute to American suburbia. There is, however, literature of a favorable nature, too. See, for example, L. E. White, "Participation of Families in the Organisation and Development of Local Communities in New Towns," *British Housing and Planning Review*, May–June 1961, pp. 9–11.

20. *Report of the Ministry of Housing and Local Government*, 1960 (London: HMSO, 1961), p. 96.

21. This will be true of Canada as well as the United States. See E. G. Faludi, "Designing New Canadian Communities, Theory and Practice," *Journal of the American Institute of Planners*, Spring 1950, p. 78.

22. This type of land utilization and planning is still unusual

in American developments. For example: "What makes Crofton unique in the country is the extent to which it was finished before houses were put on sale . . . Among the completed features [before sales] were two entrance gates with winding, landscaped entrance roads, a Village Green with a dozen finished buildings, an 18th Century tavern, a year-round recreation building, a swimming pool, a golf Pro shop, an 18-hole, championship golf course, six furnished models, an exhibit center, several miles of paved streets, several hundred gas lights, four parking lots, several acres of sodded public areas. A group of town houses was under construction. Even after the dryest summer in 20 years, Crofton looked green and beautiful. Everything seemed to have been there a long time. Completely absent was the scorched earth look that is typical of so many construction jobs." Carl Norcross, "A Look at Crofton, Maryland—New Ideas in Creating a Fine Environment," *Urban Land*, December 1964, pp. 3–4.

23. "Mass Builder Levitt Becomes a Marketer as Buyers Get Choosy," *Wall Street Journal*, Dec. 4, 1964, p. 1.

24. For a concise description of Reston, see "Reston: An Answer to Urban Sprawl: Urban Living in the Country," *Architectural Record*, July 1964, pp. 119–134. For a more recent account, see "Reston Starts Year 2000 Plan," *Engineering News-Record*, Jan. 29, 1965, pp. 53–56.

25. For an interesting analysis of Columbia, see J. W. Anderson, "A Brand New City for Maryland—A Big, Bold Dream in the Making," *Harper's Magazine*, November 1964, pp. 100–106. Additional accounts of new communities in the United States, which refer to the movement rather than one particular development, include Ada Louise Huxtable, "First Light of New Town Era Is on Horizon," *New York Times*, Feb. 17, 1964, and Robert W. Murray, Jr., "New Towns for America," *House and Home*, February 1964, pp. 123–131.

26. "Reston: An Answer," as cited in my note 24.

27. In Canada, too, where new towns are developed by private enterprise, they have failed, despite their initial hopes, to include all economic classes. Faludi (as cited in my note 21), pp. 78–79.

28. Bernard Weissbourd, *Segregation, Subsidies, and Megalopolis*, Occasional Paper No. 1 on the City (Santa Barbara, Cal.:

Center for the Study of Democratic Institutions, 1964), p. 7. This writer affirms (p. 8) that "only a major plan to induce a substantial part of the Negro working population to live in outlying 'new towns' can bring about a more uniform and just distribution of these people among the population as a whole."

29. Wolf Von Eckardt, "The Community: Could This Be Our Town?" *New Republic*, Nov. 7, 1964, p. 21.

30. Carl Norcross (cited in note 22, above), p. 4.

31. Catherine Bauer Wurster, "The Form and Structure of the Future Urban Complex," in *Cities and Space: The Future Use of Urban Land*, ed. Lowdon Wingo, Jr. (Baltimore: Johns Hopkins Press, 1963), pp. 76–77, 95.

32. Giorgio Gentili, *The Satellite Towns of Stockholm* (Stockholm: Department of Planning and Building Control, 1960), p. 5. The official position of the Department of Planning and Building Control of Stockholm is that Vallingby and other suburban groups were never planned to be self-supporting satellite towns (Goran Sidenbadh, in the foreword to the article cited, p. 2).

33. John Hillaby, "8,000-Year-Old 'City Plan' Dug Up at Turkish Site," *New York Times*, Dec. 18, 1964, p. 12.

CHAPTER 3: URBAN RENEWAL

1. Martin Anderson, *The Federal Bulldozer* (Cambridge, Mass.: M.I.T. Press, 1964). There are many reviews of this book, some of which are cited subsequently. For an analysis of the unbalanced and faulty statistical methods of Anderson, see Frank S. Kristof, "Challenges Critical View of Urban Renewal," *Savings Bank Journal*, April 1965, pp. 36–39.

2. Chester W. Hartman, "The Housing of Relocated Families," *Journal of the American Institute of Planners*, November 1964, pp. 266–286.

3. James Q. Wilson, "Urban Renewal Does Not Always Renew," *Harvard Today*, January 1965, pp. 2–3.

4. "Fiction, Heresy and Housing," *Wall Street Journal*, March 4, 1965, p. 18. Another periodical serves as an illustration of how Mr. Wilson is cited as a critic of urban renewal. This says his "comments, like those of a growing number of recent critics of the . . . program, suggest that the huge Federal payouts for

22. For example, see G. Holmes Perkins, "New Towns for America's Peacetime Needs," *Journal of the American Institute of Architects*, January 1951, pp. 11–15.

23. Schaller, cited in my note 6, p. 3.

24. One of the roots of this confusion seems to lie in the fact that housing legislation and federal housing policy have as their objective a decent home and a suitable living environment for every American family. Because this was the national goal of the act which established urban renewal, many writers in the field have assumed that it is the goal of the urban renewal program, *per se*, ignoring the fact that housing legislation has long been in the form of an omnibus bill, containing other specific provisions for increasing the supply of housing. See, for example, Grigsby, cited above in my note 9, pp. 323–331.

25. James W. Rouse and Nathaniel S. Keith, *No Slums in Ten Years, A Workable Program for Urban Renewal*, Report to the Commissioners of the District of Columbia, January 1955.

26. For a description of this development, see "Southwest Washington: Finest Urban Renewal Effort in the Country," *Architectural Forum*, January 1963, pp. 85–90.

27. The literature on urban renewal abounds with descriptions of the West End of Boston and generalizations which assume that it was a typical American slum. For an instance of this in an otherwise scientific analysis, see Marc Fried and Peggy Gleicher, "Some Sources of Residential Satisfaction in an Urban Slum," *Journal of the American Institute of Planners*, November 1961, pp. 305–315. Hartman, too, based his earlier conclusions relative to relocation, cited in my note 2, upon a study of the West End of Boston which was published in 1959.

28. These observations are based upon a survey made for the Housing and Home Finance Agency by the U.S. Bureau of the Census, cited in my note 33, below.

29. One of the most significant is John W. Dyckman and Reginald R. Isaacs, *Capital Requirements for Urban Development and Renewal* (New York: McGraw-Hill, 1961), a volume in the ACTION Series in Housing and Community Development.

30. For a more detailed discussion of the filtering process, see my *The Urban Complex*, pp. 50–51.

31. Even if these students of urban renewal hesitate to resort

to "conventional wisdom," they chose carefully their data. As in the case of Hartman, cited above in note 2, they concentrate upon the earlier experience which admittedly was reprehensible. At least Hartman cited more recent data, although he ignored them in his analysis. Wilson fails even to do this. In his article which post-dates Hartman's piece, he cites only studies in the late 1950's (Wilson, cited above, my note 3). In a more current article Hartman is a little less bearish, citing Urban Renewal Administration reports that 80 percent of the program's dislocated families moved into decent, safe, and sanitary dwellings. He and a co-author reiterate the observation that political pressures on local public agencies tend to render their relocation figures "unrealistically optimistic . . . the true figure may well be under eighty per cent." William W. Nash, Jr., and Chester W. Hartman, "Laissez-Faire in the Slums," *The Reporter*, Feb. 25, 1965, p. 49.

32. Weaver, *The Urban Complex*, p. 103.

33. *The Housing of Relocated Families* (Washington: Housing and Home Finance Agency, March 1965).

34. *Ibid.*, pp. 6–9.

35. Anderson points this out, although by ignoring the time sequences he grossly overstates the issue. *The Federal Bulldozer*, pp. 163–172.

36. For a description of the Section 221(d)(3) program, see Weaver, *The Urban Complex*, pp. 85–86, 114–118, 126, 252–254.

37. For example: "Urban renewal has been used to increase the city's tax base, 'stabilize' the city's population, to beautify the city's face, to polish the city's image. It has not often been used to help those people of the city who need help most . . . urban renewal must be expanded, not cut back, but it must be expanded in its objectives as well as its extent. It must be directed at the rehabilitation of the urban poor, particularly the urban minorities, as well as the redevelopment of their dwellings." Donald Canty, "Architecture and the Urban Emergency," *Architectural Forum*, August–September 1964, pp. 173–178.

38. "Little-Used Law Aids Remodeling," *New York Times*, Feb. 7, 1965, sec. 8, p. 1.

39. For a more detailed analysis of rehabilitation, see M. Carter McFarland, *The Challenge of Urban Renewal*, Technical Bulletin No. 34 (Washington: Urban Land Institute, 1962), pp. 25–34,

and "Residential Rehabilitation," in *Pioneering Urban Land Economics*, ed. James Gillies (Los Angeles: University of California Press, 1965).

40. For an account of urban renewal programs in New Haven and Boston which reflect these new directives, see William Lee Miller and L. Thomas Appleby, " 'You Shove Out the Poor to Make Houses for the Rich,' " *New York Times Magazine*, April 11, 1965, which starts on p. 36, and John P. Reardon, "Urban Renewal—Another Look," *Harvard Today*, Spring 1965, pp. 2–6.

41. "New Spirit of St. Louis Sparks Renaissance," *Engineering News-Record*, Aug. 15, 1963, which starts on p. 30; Will Lissner, "Urban Renewal Reviving Centers of Nation's Cities," *New York Times*, April 6, 1964; "The City: Under the Knife, or All for Their Own Good," *Time*, Nov. 6, 1964; "Big Cities Try for a Comeback," *U.S. News and World Report*, Dec. 28, 1964, pp. 34–38. For a more recent description of downtown urban redevelopment undertakings, with special emphasis upon their aesthetics, see "Pedestrian Malls Brighten Up Downtowns Nationwide," *Journal of Housing*, January 1965, pp. 12–13.

42. Raymond Vernon, *The Myth and Reality of Our Urban Problems* (Cambridge, Mass.: Joint Center for Urban Studies of M.I.T. and Harvard University, 1962), p. 42.

43. Charles Abrams, "Downtown Decay and Revival," *Journal of the American Institute of Planners*, February 1961, p. 9.

CHAPTER 4: DILEMMAS OF RACE

1. James Q. Wilson, "Urban Renewal Does Not Always Renew," *Harvard Today*, January 1965, p. 2.

2. Charles E. Silberman, "The City and the Negro," *Fortune*, March 1962, p. 89.

3. Lyle E. Schaller, "Urban Renewal: Is It Un-American?" *Mayor and Manager*, June 1964, p. 4.

4. Nat Hentoff, *The New Equality* (New York: Viking Press, 1964), p. 125.

5. Whitney M. Young, Jr., "Civil Rights Action and the Urban League," in *Assuring Freedom to the Free*, ed. Arnold M. Rose (Detroit: Wayne State University Press, 1964), p. 216.

6. Karl E. Taeuber, *Negro Residential Segregation, 1940–1960: Changing Trends in the Large Cities of the United States*, paper

delivered at the annual meeting of the American Sociological Association, Washington, D.C., Aug. 31, 1962 (Chicago: Population Research and Training Center, 1963), pp. 5–6.

7. William Brink and Louis Harris, *The Negro Revolution in America* (New York: Simon & Schuster, 1964), pp. 148–152. And following is a recent Gallup poll report: "More white people today than two years ago are willing to accept Negroes as next-door neighbors. In a survey in May, 1963, 45 per cent of whites across the Nation said they would definitely move—or might move—if a colored family came to live next door. Today the comparable survey figure is 35 per cent." "The Gallup Poll: Opposition to Negroes as Neighbors Decreases," *Washington Post*, May 28, 1965, p. A2.

8. "New Tithing Plan Aimed at Housing," *New York Times*, Feb. 21, 1965, sec. 8, p. 1.

9. "Home Sale Curbs Opposed in Texas," *New York Times*, March 2, 1965, p. 57.

10. Bernard Weissbourd, *Segregation, Subsidies, and Megalopolis*, Occasional Paper No. 1 on the City (Santa Barbara, Cal.: Center for the Study of Democratic Institutions, 1964), p. 7.

11. For a documentation of this in one locality, see William Lee Miller and L. Thomas Appleby, " 'You Shove Out the Poor to Make Houses for the Rich,' " *New York Times Magazine*, April 11, 1965.

12. For a discussion of income groups and fair housing committees, see George B. Nesbitt and Elfriede F. Hoeber, "The Fair Housing Committee: Its Need for a New Perspective," *Land Economics*, May 1965, pp. 97–110.

13. For an account of Chicago's experience in site selection for public housing developments, see Martin Meyerson and Edward C. Banfield, *Politics, Planning, and the Public Interest* (Glencoe, Ill.: Free Press, 1955). Recent examples of neighborhood opposition to urban renewal programs of Westchester County, N.Y., are discussed in James R. Sikes, "Newburgh Divided in Urban Renewal Plan: Integration of Negroes Is Key Issue," *New York Times*, May 7, 1965, p. 37, and Samuel Kaplan, "Yonkers Debates Slum Integration: Renewal Plan Would Shift Poor to City Projects in Top Residential Areas," *New York Times*, May 5, 1965.

14. Washington, D.C., presents an extreme example of this.

See my *The Urban Complex* (New York: Doubleday & Co., 1964), pp. 251–252.

15. *Ibid.*, p. 254.

16. *Ibid.*, pp. 131–132.

17. For a statistical summary of current income distribution of residential redevelopment, see p. 69 above.

18. Silberman (my note 2, above), p. 88.

19. *Ibid.*, p. 154.

20. See, for example, *Inner City* (Newsletter for Lutherans), January 1965, p. 5.

21. Elinor Rickey, "Keeping the Outsiders Out," *Saturday Review*, Oct. 19, 1963, pp. 22–24.

22. Baker E. Morten, "Urban Renewal Axed," *Washington Afro-American*, Feb. 13, 1965, pp. 1–2, and "The Case of Adams-Morgan," *ibid.*, p. 4.

23. "Urban Renewal Rejected for Adams-Morgan Area," *Washington Afro-American*, Feb. 6, 1965, pp. 1–2.

24. Lewis G. Watts, Howard E. Freeman, Helen M. Hughes, Robert Morris, and Thomas F. Pettigrew, *The Middle-Income Negro Family Faces Urban Renewal*, a study made by Brandeis University for the Department of Commerce and Development, Commonwealth of Massachusetts, 1964.

25. Nesbitt and Hoeber, cited in my note 12, above.

26. Miller and Appleby, cited my note 11.

27. Watts, *et al.*, cited in my note 24.

28. Kenneth B. Clark, *Dark Ghetto: Dilemmas of Social Power* (New York: Harper & Row, 1965), pp. 114–115.

CHAPTER 5: SUMMING UP

1. William W. Nash, Jr., and Chester W. Hartman, "Laissez-Faire in the Slums," *The Reporter*, Feb. 25, 1965, p. 53. James Q. Wilson made substantially the same point in his recent testimony relative to the Housing and Urban Development Act of 1965. *Hearings before the Subcommittee on Housing of the Committee on Banking and Currency, House of Representatives, 89th Cong., 1st Sess.*, April 1, 2, 5, 6, and 7, 1965 (Washington: Government Printing Office, 1965), pp. 813–815.

2. Weaver, *The Urban Complex* (New York: Doubleday & Co., 1964), p. 43.

INDEX

138   INDEX